SIDETRACKED IN THE MIDWEST

A Green Guide for Travelers

MARY BERGIN

ITCHY CAT PRESS

Library of Congress Cataloging-in-Publication Data

Bergin, Mary.
  Sidetracked in the midwest : a green guide for travelers / Mary Bergin. -- 1st ed.
      p. cm.
  Includes bibliographical references and index.
  ISBN 978-0-9815161-2-7 (alk. paper)
  1. Middle West--Guidebooks. 2. Ecotourism--Middle West--Guidebooks. I. Title.
  F350.3.B46 2011
  977--dc22
                            2011002151

ITCHY CAT PRESS
Blue Mounds
Wisconsin 53517 USA
608.924.1443
www.itchycatpress.com
ffg@mhtc.net

front cover: Monona Terrace Community and Convention Center, Madison, Wisconsin

back cover, top: Honey Creek Resort's lobby, Moravia, Iowa

   bottom: A thick carpet of purple salvia at Lurie Garden, Chicago, Illinois
preceding page, top: Bulbous tree growths at entryway to Legs Inn, Cross Village, Michigan

   bottom: Lunch in the barn at Pond Hill Farm, Harbor Springs, Michigan

Designed and produced by Flying Fish Graphics   Printed in Canada

To the many inquisitive, conscientious and compassionate minds at Madison's First Unitarian Society—thriving through the smart and steady leadership of the Reverend Michael A. Schuler.

Keep the faith, however you define it.

CONTENTS

INTRODUCTION

I like a good challenge, but the notion of producing a book about Midwest ecotourism seemed paralyzing for quite a while. Where to begin? What to include? Whose criteria rule?

Ecotourism standards change, enthusiasm mushrooms and expectations increase as I write this. LEED certification, for example, isn't just about buildings anymore. Now this internationally respected benchmark extends to neighborhoods.

The addition of in-room recycling bins in hotels and menus with locally grown foods in restaurants no longer are avant-garde moves, but neither should the value of these efforts be diminished. It's all good—tiny steps to multi-million dollar investments.

"Going green" suggests a respect for nature, selfless choices, environment above ego. How our endeavors play out continue to surprise and delight us. We're green with envy and hope about the various projects that compete for attention.

So many paths are new, with myriad ways to measure progress. A nod from the U.S. Green Building Council is one measurement of eco-progressive-ness, but other efforts count, too. That includes reusing what's old instead of discarding it.

I admire developers who refurbish old buildings for creative purposes instead of simply demolishing them. The same goes for the rural innkeeper who lovingly shares simple, off-the-grid lodging—and the upscale B&B owner who agonizes about the eco-impact of the tiniest details of business.

As with my previous books, *Sidetracked in Wisconsin* and *Hungry for Wisconsin*, I consider the best mix of content to be eclectic.

Low-budget to luxury projects, in rural to densely populated areas, make the cut in four categories: food/drink, lodging/retreats, nature/wildlife, the old and the new. Eco features will be evident to the average traveler.

I try to not brag too much about my beloved Madison, home to fervent food activists, a maze of bike trails and a progressive bike-sharing system, mandatory plastic bag recycling and the nation's largest producer-only farmers' market (all vendors also are the producers of what is sold).

I'll mention, but not dwell on, the fact that ideas and action about conservation certainly aren't new in my home state of

Wisconsin, thanks to native sons Aldo Leopold, John Muir, Gaylord Nelson and other trailblazers.

What I present in *Sidetracked in the Midwest* is a range of possibilities, examples of people who are running with inventive ideas that involve many types of businesses. But don't consider it the last word about ecotourism in the Midwest. The discussion—and work—has only just begun.

—*Mary Bergin*

ABOUT THE AUTHOR

Mary Bergin of Madison, Wisconsin, grew up on a farm within sight of the Sheboygan County Marsh, a 14,000-acre wildlife area near the outskirts of the Kettle Moraine State Forest. The farmland has reverted to its natural state and today is a part of the marsh, managed by the Wisconsin Department of Natural Resources.

The author is a fan of resale shops, independently owned businesses, farmers' markets and eating most meals at home. Her humble vegetable garden struggles inside of containers. She seeks public transportation instead of car rentals when traveling, and she's never driven a car in Chicago because she prefers keeping her sanity and boarding a Metra train.

TERMINOLOGY

Carbon footprint. The level of greenhouse gas emissions that an activity causes.

CSA. An abbreviation for Community Supported Agriculture, an arrangement whereby the consumer pays upfront one price for one share of a farmer's seasonal harvest. The food typically is distributed weekly during the growing season.

LEED. An abbreviation for Leadership in Energy and Environmental Design, the U.S. Green Building Council's benchmark for measuring sustainability in building design, construction and operation.

LEED ratings. Indications of a structure's level of sustainability. A LEED platinum certification is the highest rating achievable, followed by gold and silver.

Net-zero energy. When a project creates as much or more energy than it uses.

Off the grid. Not requiring connection to public utilities.

Sustainability. Practices that protect and enhance natural and human resources.

SIDETRACKED IN THE MIDWEST

A Green Guide for Travelers

This book is arranged by state, with maps and page numbers to help
you find green lodges and retreats, restaurants, nature centers, renovated
buildings with new purposes, off-the-grid escapes. Sometimes small towns
trump large cities, or gems pop up in unexpected places. Have fun exploring,
but remember to call before you begin driving. Business operation details are
subject to change.

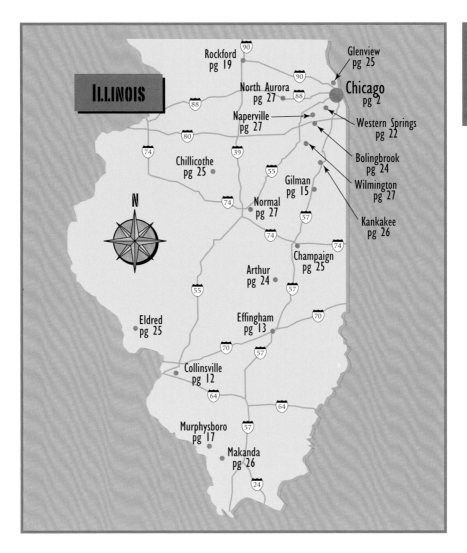

ILLINOIS

Rockford
pg 19

Glenview
pg 25

North Aurora
pg 27

Chicago
pg 2

Naperville
pg 27

Western Springs
pg 22

Chillicothe
pg 25

Bolingbrook
pg 24

Gilman
pg 15

Wilmington
pg 27

N

Normal
pg 27

Kankakee
pg 26

Champaign
pg 25

Arthur
pg 24

Eldred
pg 25

Effingham
pg 13

Collinsville
pg 12

Murphysboro
pg 17

Makanda
pg 26

Meet passionate people who envision a greater good. A culinary school makes lessons in sustainability a teaching priority. A green retreat rises on worn-out land. Seeds for self-improvement sprout at a rural destination spa.

DANA HOTEL
Chicago, Illinois

You might not think that raw concrete ceilings and exposed pipes belong in a luxury property, but think again. Three blocks west of Chicago's Magnificent Mile is boutique lodging that is locally owned and environmentally conscious.

Recycled and reclaimed wood, glass and other materials show that "plush" need not mean thick carpeting or a ton of incidental accoutrements. Windows in some guest rooms open, so bring on the fresh air.

Spa flooring is recycled beer bottles. Room cards are recycled PVC. Mr. Kites, a Chicago candy and nut business, provides little bags of snacks, but prices aren't what you'd expect in the big city. You can get an in-room fix of caramels, toffee or chocolate for less than $5 or open a bottle of wine for less than $20.

WiFi, local calls and a newspaper are free. Chocolate-dipped fortune cookies from Mr. Kites appear on bed pillows at night.

For an unusual thrill, head to the rooftop in winter, when 500 pounds of ice forms a bar. The bartender wears a parka, and you can sit around a fire pit wrapped in a cozy robe from the hotel. The hotel restaurant specializes in simple, regional Asian cooking that draws from local and sustainable fare.

The vibe is stylish, but if you're not, it doesn't much matter. "Eclectic" décor doesn't mean pretentious attitude. You'll see

Recycled materials are stylish at Dana Hotel.

staffers welcome the hip, happenin' and has-beens. After all, "dana" is Sanskrit for "the pleasure of giving." LEED certification is being pursued.

Dana Hotel and Spa
660 N. State Street
Chicago, Illinois
www.danahotelandspa.com 888-301-7952

•

Friendly greeter at Hotel Felix

Also in the neighborhood:

Hotel Felix, 111 W. Huron Street, in 2010 was Chicago's first hotel to earn LEED silver certification. On the long list of ecological practices: Wind turbines on the roof generate renewable energy. Hybrid vehicles get free parking. No bleach is used anywhere on the property. Cork and bamboo cover floors in public areas.

www.hotelfelixchicago.com
877-848-4040

•

Chicago celebrity chef Rick Bayless, whose restaurant empire—especially **Frontera Grill**, 445 N. Clark Street—never seems to have an off night or vacant tables, long ago sought the products of family farms to enrich his menus. He certainly isn't alone in this mission, but gets extra points for sincerity because of his Frontera Farmer Foundation, a nonprofit that awards grants to small and sustainable farms in need of help.

www.rickbayless.com 312-661-1434

Their homework will satisfy your appetite.

KENDALL COLLEGE:
THE DINING ROOM

Chicago, Illinois

Time it right at Kendall College, and one person's final exam is your scrumptious, good-looking and good-deal meal.

Eating someone else's homework can be a pleasure, when it happens at the college's culinary arts program, which has about 700 enrollees. Fine dining at subsidized prices gives tomorrow's chefs real-life experience.

I got my taste of it during a Grand Buffet, an event that tests the talents of 12 to 18 culinary students. They prepare *garde manger*: patés, mousses, terrines and other fancy nibbles for appetizer platters. Instructors evaluate taste, technique, appearance, creativity and execution of theme.

"I put a lot of deadlines into their work," says Pierre Checchi, chef instructor. That prepares students for real-life situations.

"We have a reputation for being tough on our students," echoes Christopher Koetke, culinary program dean. "The students who thrive on the challenge are going to take on the industry."

So standards are high and the public benefits. One student's contribution included curry smoked chicken salad, served on crackers with Indian spices. Another presented a rabbit and venison terrine, plus crostini topped with spicy goat cheese and a vegetable tapenade.

The *garde manger* is complemented by a small selection of hot entrées (such as pastas) and a dessert table. Students also wait on tables, and all are being graded as they work.

"When you eat here, you are taking part in the education of the students," says the dean, who estimates that actual costs are roughly twice what customers pay for a meal.

The culinary arts work gains national and international awards for sustainability. Environmental stewardship means recycling, conserving, composting and more.

A college-produced video extends these teachings to the food service industry. A Kendall garden grows food for its restaurant meals and teaches students the principles of sustainable agriculture.

Check out the exhibits of antique cooking equipment; artifacts are up to 500 years old. Fixed-price and à la carte menus for lunch and dinner are available on most days. Reservations are necessary.

The Dining Room at Kendall College is one of only three Michelin-recognized culinary schools in the U.S., and Kendall was the nation's first culinary school to earn Green Restaurant Association certification.

The Dining Room, Kendall College
900 N. North Branch Street
Chicago, Illinois
www.kendall.edu 312-752-2328
•

The Chicago skyline makes a wonderful backdrop to Lurie Garden.

LURIE GARDEN
Chicago, Illinois

Spring had just arrived, and the last snow had barely melted. What would there be to see in a garden in northern Illinois? I had come to Millennium Park to see one of the world's largest rooftop gardens, which thrives on its perch atop a mass transit station and parking garages.

Odd and alluring outdoor sculptures—like the bright silver Cloud Gate ("The Bean"), whose reflection stretches and twists the cityscape—distinguish this urban park from others. So does the five-acre Lurie Garden because of its low-maintenance, sustainable design. It is a tranquil respite from big-city bustle and a magnet for more than four million visitors per year.

"We see a lot of interest, even in winter, because of the habitat this area provides for birds," says Jennifer Davit, the garden's chief horticulturist. Foliage is not cut back, so dustings of frost or snow add subtle to dramatic visual effects.

Jennifer is one of two paid staff who tend Lurie Garden. Ten volunteers help garden, and another 40 lead tours and workshops throughout the year.

Most of the plantings are perennials arranged carefully to lessen runoff and the need for mass irrigation. Volunteers plant 120,000 flower bulbs in early May.

"Color was really the last thing that the designers looked at," Jennifer says, of the garden layout. "It's about variations in texture and height, and how the plants interact with each other in the bed."

Hedges, which share a "Big Shoulders" nickname with Chicago, protect and enclose two sides of the area, creating a natural buffer against city sounds and a microclimate conducive to plant growth. The garden's slight slope enhances water flow. Many plants will grow head high, so you feel immersed in surroundings.

An elevated wooden path, suspended over shallow water, divides the garden's sunny and shaded areas, which staff and designers refer to as the light and dark plates. The latter takes on an intentionally rougher and wilder appearance.

"We're a good urban demo garden that shows what gardeners can do at their own home," Jennifer says. She is referring, in part, to the native plants that take up the majority of garden space and provide attractive habitat for wildlife. Her goal is to "promote the garden as a destination in itself." Admission is free, with free tours on some days.

For an excellent elevated view, follow a pedestrian bridge from the garden to the Modern Wing of the Art Institute of Chicago.

Lurie Garden and Millennium Park
Michigan Avenue, between Randolph and Monroe Streets
Chicago, Illinois
www.luriegarden.org www.millenniumpark.com
312-742-1168
•

Each sea otter at the Shedd eats 2,000-plus pounds of shrimp per year.

SHEDD AQUARIUM
Chicago, Illinois

How do you feed a voracious crowd of 32,000, every day of every year? When you're doing meal prep for aquatic occupants at the Shedd, one menu does not serve all—especially since staff aim to design healthy diets that simultaneously go easy on the Earth.

Plants in some of the aquarium's lush gardens are specifically grown and snipped to feed lizards, turtles and some of the fish. Shrimp-like mysids, fruit flies, water fleas, micro-algae and other food also are raised on the premises.

Meeting dietary needs also poses challenges; consider the five Alaska sea otters that eat 12,000 pounds of shrimp per year. Using the Shedd as the food incubator is unrealistic, but aquarium staff also know that most shrimp are not sustainably caught or farmed.

Shrimp trawling nets catch—and kill—an alarming amount of other wildlife and destroy habitats. The typical shrimp farm uses additives—antibiotics, preservatives—in water to keep its catch disease-free.

Research led the diet-conscious Shedd to a small farm in Arizona that goes against these conventional methods to produce shrimp. So now much of the farm's work is devoted to raising shrimp that meet the aquarium's feeding requirements.

The Shedd's commitment to sustainable seafood—that which is raised naturally and harvested in ways that do not deplete aquatic populations—extends to people, too. The Right Bite seafood wallet card, which can be downloaded for free online, shows which seafood species are abundant and tend to be raised or harvested in eco-friendly ways.

You'll see it's fine to eat U.S. farmed tilapia but not the Asian farmed variety. Wild Alaskan salmon is a better choice than most types that are farmed. Pacific halibut gets a thumbs-up, but not that which comes from the Atlantic.

Whole Foods Market works with the aquarium to select a Fish of the Month and provide recipes for preparing it. Too busy to cook? Order the Fish of the Month lunch special at the Shedd's Soundings Cafe.

Shedd Aquarium
1200 S. Lake Shore Drive
Chicago, Illinois
www.sheddaquarium.org, 312-939-2438
•

One of the most popular areas for children at the Shedd's enlarged Oceanarium is the Penguin Play Area. The challenge to "be a penguin" means sliding down a faux ice slide, putting on a penguin vest and wings, carrying around penguin-sized eggs and crawling through pint-sized caverns.

All happens within eyesight of real penguins, which makes you wonder which species ends up more amused or confused.

More green places to visit in Chicago:

Scientists and volunteers at the **Peggy Notebaert Nature Museum**, 2430 N. Cannon Drive, carefully monitor endangered Blanding's turtles. The museum provides a safe place for the shells of hatchlings to grow hard, so they can be released into protected wildlife areas. The museum also makes restoration of rare native butterfly populations a priority.

www.naturemuseum.org 773-755-5100

•

Architectural Artifacts, Inc., 4325 N. Ravenswood Street, is developing a free museum of Windy City artifacts created by Frank Lloyd Wright, Louis Sullivan and other masters of architectural design. Look for the new, 15,000-square-foot Museum of Historic Chicago Architecture in the 50-foot-tall atrium of this one-of-a-kind business.

www.architecturalartifacts.com 773-348-0622

•

Peonies at the Lurie Garden

Midwest farmers, many toting specialty products, fill **Green City Market** at the south end of Lincoln Park on Wednesdays and Saturdays during the growing season. When winter approaches, sales move inside the Peggy Notebaert Nature Museum. Look for chef cooking demos and activities for children.

www.chicagogreencitymarket.org 773-880-1266

•

Bobby's Bike Hike Chicago since 1992 has taken tourists for a ride during all times of year, using bicycle paths, sidewalks and parks to get acquainted with the city's lakefront, Gold Coast mansions, Lincoln Park Zoo and neighborhoods. The narrated tours take two to three hours; take the little ones on the Tike Hike, which includes a trivia contest (with prizes). Departure points depend upon the itinerary.

www.bobbysbikehike.com 312-915-0995

•

In the **Green Chicago Restaurant Co-op** are nearly two dozen restaurants that declare their commitment to environmentally responsible business practices. All also belong to the Green Restaurant Association. In the group are **avec**, 615 W. Randolph Street; **Big Jones**, 5347 N. Clark Street; **Blackbird**, 619 W. Randolph Street; **Bleeding Heart Bakery**, 1955 W. Belmont Avenue; **Blind Faith Cafe**, 525 Dempster Street, Evanston; **The Dining Room at Kendall College**, 900 N. North Branch Street; **Frontera Grill**, 445 N. Clark Street; **Hannah's Bretzel**, 233 N. Michigan Avenue; **Keefer's**, 20 W. Kinzie Street; **Poag Mahone's**, 333 S. Wells Street; **The Publican**, 837 W. Fulton Market; **Roti Mediterranean Grill**, 10 S. Riverside Plaza; **Simone's Bar**, 960 W. 18th Street; **Sopraffina Marketcaffe**, 111 E. Wacker Drive, 200 E. Randolph Drive, 10 N. Dearborn Street, 222 W. Adams Street and 175 W. Jackson Boulevard; **Topolobampo**, 445 N. Clark Street; **Trattoria No. 10**, 10 N. Dearborn Street; and **Uncommon Ground**, 1401 W. Devon Avenue and 3800 N. Clark Street.

www.buygreenchicago.com

CAHOKIA MOUNDS

Collinsville, Illinois

A Native American culture—the largest pre-Columbian settlement north of Mexico—lived here from around AD 700 to 1400. The site takes up 2,200 acres and has been a UNESCO World Heritage Site since 1982.

Cahokia was larger than London in the year 1250 and its population peaked at around 20,000. There apparently was no larger city in the United States until 1800, when Philadelphia's population surpassed it.

Had this agricultural community used building materials that would withstand prolonged exposure—like the limestone of Mexico's Chichen Itza or the granite of Peru's Machu Picchu—Cahokia Mounds would be as well known. Only wall trenches and post holes remain as evidence of the homes made of wood and dirt here long ago.

The Cahokia tribe built more than 120 mounds, some enlarged several times. Monks Mound, at 100 feet high, took 300 years to build and is the largest prehistoric earthwork in the Americas. Only 80 of the original 120 mounds still exist, and their shapes explain their purpose. Temples and homes of leaders, for example, were built on top of platform-shaped mounds; the chief lived on the highest. Conical mounds, some rising 40 feet, were for the burial of important people.

Cahokia's decline in the late thirteenth or early fourteenth century came slowly. Poor nutrition and disease were factors, but much about why and how the community vanished remains a mystery.

On the site is an interpretive center with dioramas that show early life as reconstructed by archaeologists. Learn more through a film, one-hour guided tours, and strolling the grounds.

Cahokia Mounds State Historic Site
30 Ramey Street
Collinsville, Illinois
www.cahokiamounds.org 618-346-5160
•

Enjoy fresh pizza at one of the nation's top eco-friendly restaurants.

FIREFLY GRILL

Effingham, Illinois

Snip, snip. There goes more fresh mint for a mojito, plus a couple of peppery flower blossoms for the next entrée's garnish. It is not unusual to see staff walk outside to harvest ingredients as they are needed.

A part of kitchen duty at Firefly Grill involves tending a two-acre garden that is next to the restaurant, on the edge of a community of 20,000 and at the busy junction of Highways 57 and 70.

When Firefly Grill began in 2006, so did the garden. Brussels sprouts, bok choy, assorted types of squash, lettuce, hot peppers and tomatoes nearly fill the smartly seeded garden plot. Some plants are heirloom varieties. "What we don't grow, we get from local farms," says Cara Milewski, general manager.

At the peak of harvest, 75 percent of the vegetables used in the restaurant come from this space, which is irrigated by a manmade pond, to lessen water waste. Buy a handful of food to toss to the pond's catfish, bass, koi and bluegill; all proceeds benefit a local no-kill animal shelter.

When we visit, the roadhouse menu of six-dollar lunch specials boasts almost a dozen choices. Top seller, during midsummer: caprese salad, the dreamy mix of fresh tomatoes, mozzarella and basil.

Oak-fired steaks (including elk ribeyes) and brick-oven pizzas are specialties. Our squash blossom arrives stuffed with an herb-flavored chevre. Then come fried green tomatoes.

What's behind the name? Co-owner and Effingham native Kristie Campbell recalled her grandmother's house, where fireflies brightened the backyard. Kristie's husband, chef Niall, is responsible for development of the heartland cuisine.

Recycled barn wood, refurbished stainless steel, locally produced artwork and Campbell wedding photos define the restaurant's structure and décor. We eat on butcher block tables that are not covered with linens, and our chairs came from Manhattan's Hard Rock Cafe.

In 2008 *Bon Appetit* chose Firefly Grill as one of the nation's top ten eco-friendly restaurants.

Firefly Grill
1810 Mid America Avenue
Effingham, Illinois
www.ffgrill.com 217-342-2002
•

*What looks like an average farm actually is a destination spa
that nurtures self-improvement.*

HEARTLAND SPA

Gilman, Illinois

No need to pack a lot when heading to the Heartland Spa, a converted dairy farm 85 miles south of Chicago—far enough away to be considered the country.

"T-shirts, sweatpants, robes—we provide the clothes for you to wear," says Kim Onnen, fitness manager. "It's a nonjudgmental approach that makes everyone equal."

All guests receive a 7 a.m. wakeup call, and a two-mile walk typically precedes breakfast. Then come classes (such as pilates, a cooking demo or stress management), lunch, more classes and group discussion time, dinner, a lecture or tai chi with meditation. The day ends around 8 p.m.

A staff of up to 72 people, including bereavement, fitness and nutrition counselors, address needs and goals of their customers, who pay as much as $1,900 to stay here for five days. One-night rates begin at $370.

Heartland Spa has room for up to 32 people in its 16 pleasant bed-rooms. Roommates are assigned to single travelers who don't want to pay for a private room.

Inside the former dairy barn are spa services and exercise equipment. Exercise stations along a quarter-mile outdoor track encourage stretching and strengthening. There are yoga classes, weight machines, bicycles and a high ropes challenge course.

A pond on the premises is big enough for a paddleboat. Elsewhere is a meditation garden.

In winter, cross-country skiing is popular.

The typical customer is in her forties or fifties, but men and other ages are welcome. So are the morbidly obese who seek coaching to improve their habits and health; some stay as long as six weeks.

On hallway walls are slogans of inspiration, such as "Sing—music is an outburst of the soul."

The house provides only one television set. Guests do not have e-mail access and are asked to not use cell phones in common areas. A sign at the driveway entrance says No Junk Food, and guest meals are mostly vege-tarian. A welcome snack in midsummer includes passion tea, figs and slim kabobs of berries.

Heartland Spa
1237 E. 1600 North Road
Gilman, Illinois
www.heartlandspa.com 800-545-4853
•

In Liz's herd are rescued horses of varying size and circumstance.

GREEN RETREAT
Murphysboro, Illinois

This is what Liz Robinson, an acupuncturist and massage therapist, learned about the wealthy when she worked in Miami: The rich go to Aruba or Bora Bora for a vacation. The richer go to Iowa or Arkansas, to watch somebody cut hay.

She and her husband, Mike, moved back to the Midwest in 2006 with the intention of developing an eco-friendly retreat because they believed the market was green for this type of getaway. They found property near her mother's house.

"The land was in a shambles," Liz recalls. A 300-acre family farm had been divvied up and sold. Their 97 acres had cornfields, a deteriorating hay barn and cow pastures overrun by honey locust and other invasive species. "My husband could see through the brush and dirty cow puddle ponds and said, 'This will work nicely,'" she says.

Up went a geothermal steel office building and machine shop, then two houses, three cabins, a greenhouse with potting shed and an 11-stall horse stable with classroom. They stocked an 11-acre lake and ponds with fish.

"Frogs and salamanders—indicator animals, those that disappear when an environment is toxic—are here in spades," Liz says. Great blue heron "come to terrorize the fish," as do bald eagles. Forests buffer three sides of their property, 30 acres of which are going into conservation status.

There is a five-bedroom bed and breakfast (with event center and performance kitchen, for cooking demos). The retreat presents a wide range of lodging, meant to attract families on tight budgets as well as gatherings for corporate executives.

The plush and private Tree House, which resembles a three-story chalet, sleeps four. At the other extreme are the compact cabins, with queen or bunk beds and kitchenette. B&B options include quarters appropriate for people who travel with a personal attendant.

The retreat's "horse hotel" accommodates people who travel with horses. Other horse lovers can follow the owners' herd, which include registered paint horses, used-up thoroughbreds, rescued carnival animals and others that had been abused. A few can be ridden, but only by experienced riders.

"They're a draw that is special, especially for children," Liz says. "I call them my big dogs behind the fence." The fencing is electrically charged through solar power, and is moved easily, so grazing areas change often.

"Anybody from anywhere in the world should feel comfortable here," Liz says. "That's our goal. We want people to come here and experience technologies and our local culture."

Liz describes this part of Illinois as "a mix of almost-Appalachian isolationists and rural towns, but also with sophisticated art and subculture scenes." A southern Illinois wine trail begins near here. Nature preserves, national forests, and Revolutionary and Civil War battle sites are nearby, as is the Cherokee Trail of Tears.

"Seeing a fish jump or a frog get its dinner makes for a rich, common experience. If kids are picking out pumpkins, we'll help weigh and measure them—sneak in all kinds of little lessons" about nature, says Liz.

Green Retreat
6096 Chautauqua Road
Murphysboro, Illinois
www.greenretreat.com 618-687-1717
•

ANDERSON JAPANESE GARDENS

Rockford, Illinois

Diners overlook an elegant garden setting rated best in America.

Anderson Japanese Gardens is a 12-acre haven of cool green tranquility. The careful arrangement of waterfalls, bridges, ponds with colorful koi, a teahouse and many nooks with benches has earned the garden national recognition. The *Roth Journal of Japanese Gardening* rates it the best in North America.

Anderson's designer was a student of an esteemed longtime Japanese landscaper. Unusual textures and shapes play more of an aesthetic role than color—until leaves change in autumn.

Enjoy the gardens at a slow, contemplative pace. A museum-quality guest house is patterned after sixteenth-century Sukiya. Guided garden tours can be arranged.

The gift shop offers unusual merchandise that is of particular interest to gardeners and fans of Asian culture. New in 2011 is the addition of Mary's Market Cafe, a fast-casual eatery known for its from-scratch cooking and baking.

Anderson Japanese Gardens
318 Spring Creek Road
Rockford, Illinois
www.andersongardens.org 815-229-9390
•

Cliffbreakers showcases eclectic architectural paraphernalia from ages past.

CLIFFBREAKERS RIVERSIDE RESORT

Rockford, Illinois

In the Cliffbreakers' entrance is a conspicuous Italian Bazzanti fountain from the 1840s. An oak archway with mahogany embellishment comes from a courtroom in Freeport, Illinois. Door surrounds, moldings, leaded doors, brass doors, stained-glass windows, fireplaces and murals—all high-quality materials and exquisite craftsmanship—formerly sat in homes owned by Vanderbilts, Mortons, Studebakers, Fords and an unnamed Milwaukee beer baron.

Tufted parlor benches were moved from the Astor in Manhattan. Five matching crystal chandeliers hung at the Claridge in Paris.

In the dining room is the Baldachino, a carved walnut ticket booth from New York City's Grand Central Station. A hundred feet of carved marble railing came from Barclay's Bank in London.

Glazed terra cotta lions lived at the McCormick mansion in Chicago until 1953. A carved maple mantelpiece, with beveled mirror, used to belong to songwriter Cole Porter.

More than 300 antiques and unusual architectural artifacts make Cliffbreakers Riverside Resort a one-of-a-kind destination.

Collector Jimmy Vitale, now retired, wove this unusual blend of remnants into his restaurant and banquet design, then added a 105-room hotel and more dining space.

Jimmy "amassed a tremendous collection from around the world," observes Michael Ellis, who now owns the property, which overlooks the Rock River. Many of the relics were purchased during auctions or estate sales, when grand buildings were in the midst of remodeling or near demolition.

The complete and original interior of Fauerbach Brewery Beer Hall (from Madison, Wisconsin) is here. That includes wall benches stuffed with horse hair, stained-glass light fixtures, an eight-foot oak beer barrel.

A nineteenth-century Russian samovar (used to heat water) with 12 bronze taps has been made into a table lamp. This artifact and others were part of the long-closed Wagon Wheel, a resort near Rockton, Illinois, whose customers included Bob Hope and Ronald Reagan.

It all makes Cliffbreakers almost as much of a museum as it is a getaway for a meal or overnight stay. Ask for a walking tour brochure at the registration desk.

The premiere Sultan Suite—five rooms with rare pecan, ebony and ivory handcrafted furnishings—is at the high end of accommodations. Jimmy Vitale outbid Cher and Wayne Newton to obtain the furnishings, which had belonged to the sultan of Morocco and were exhibited at the Paris Exhibition of 1899 (an event that also showcased the newly completed Eiffel Tower).

Lower-priced rooms at Cliffbreakers are not heavily furnished with antiques.

Cliffbreakers Riverside Resort
700 W. Riverside Boulevard
Rockford, Illinois
www.cliffbreakers.com 815-282-3033
•

"The Jar Star" and his staff pickle their own peppers and other vegetables.

VIE RESTAURANT

Western Springs, Illinois

Todd Feitl is a pastry chef, but when we meet on a weekday afternoon he is behind the bar making his first butternut squash martini. The seasonal cocktail is a blend of "squash butter," cinnamon, cloves and ginger with a shot of Crown Royal.

"Too sweet," he decides, so he'll redo the squash butter, using less sugar, and try again. Sometimes Todd's test kitchen takes him in unexpected directions, like the time he concocted a cherry liqueur that tasted like cough syrup, "but it worked fine in a sorbet."

In addition to his fondness for culinary experiment, Todd shares his boss's passion for food preservation. Vie owner Paul Virant, a *Food & Wine Magazine* Best New Chef, is nicknamed "The Jar Star" for the hundreds of containers of heirloom, pickled, sauced and juiced fruits and vegetables that fill a cool and dark, 500-square-foot storage area near his kitchen.

Twenty quarts of sauerkraut simmer as we chat, just days before Paul made his debut on *Iron Chef* (and lost to Japan native Masaharu Morimoto by only one point).

Paul buys ingredients from many family-run farms in the Midwest, but he takes the buy-local commitment one impressive step further. Vie turns into a weekly (biweekly, during winter) truck stop for distribution of CSA shares. "It's great to be able to offer this to my customers," Paul says. "The whole mission of this restaurant has evolved into a voice about how people should be eating and sourcing their food. If you commit to a CSA share, you'll want to use the food you receive."

He explains his restaurant menu as seasonal contemporary American cuisine, with western European influences and rustic flair. "You'll find nothing overly complicated," Paul insists, "just two or three ingredients working together to create something new or elevate a familiar dish."

Paul has offered in-home cooking classes, working with whatever is in the fridge. Vie's sous chef leads cooking sessions at the restaurant, teaching how to make fresh pasta, shop for seafood, and cook with the seasons.

Vie Restaurant is in an affluent community a half-hour train ride southwest from the Chicago Loop. It earned a Michelin star in 2010.

Vie Restaurant
4471 Lawn Avenue
Western Springs, Illinois
www.vierestaurant.com 708-246-2082
•

Giant City State Park Lodge was built in the 1930s and still has its charm (page 26).

MORE GREEN PLACES TO VISIT

In Arthur, Illinois, travelers can arrange to eat a meal with an Amish family in their home and learn more about their lifestyle. A restaurant meal at **Yoder's Kitchen**, 1195 E. Columbia Street, Arthur, is another option. About 4,500 Amish live in this part of central Illinois, making it the nation's fourth largest such community. Learn more at the **Amish Interpretive Center**, 125 N. Highway 425 East, Arcola, which also distributes maps to Amish-run farms and other businesses that welcome visitors.

www.amishcenter.com 888-45-AMISH

●

Hidden Oaks Nature Center, 419 Trout Farm Road, Bolingbrook, is a LEED platinum-level project on 17 wooded acres in the greater Chicago area. The building is situated between two large oak trees, each one surrounded by a deck.

www.bolingbrookparks.org 630-739-2600

●

Prairie Fruits Farm and Creamery, 4410 N. Lincoln Avenue, Champaign, grows organic fruits and vegetables but also calls itself the first farmstead cheese-making facility in Illinois. The milk from Wes Jarrell and Leslie Cooperband's grass-fed Nubian and La Mancha goats turns into small-batch chevre, two rind cheeses, a raw milk cheese with washed rind, a ricotta and seasonally produced cheeses. Some cheeses employ sheep's milk from an Amish farm. Occasional five-course dinners feature the best of the rural neighborhood's homegrown products and are preceded by farm tours.

www.prairiefruits.com
217-643-2314

•

An inviting porch at Bluffdale Farm

Three Sisters Folk Art School, 17189 N. Highway 29, Chillicothe, has classes from basketry to woodworking at Three Sisters Park, a 400-acre farm showcase for the area's agricultural heritage, particularly as it existed shortly after World War I. In place are a farmstead and chapel; the plan is to expand the site into a village.

www.threesistersfolkartschool.com 866-278-8837

•

Horses, puppies and chickens are part of the family at the 320-acre **Bluffdale Vacation Farm**, four miles north of Eldred, which has welcomed visitors since 1963. It offers dorm-like rooms, family-sized cabins with fireplaces, and hot tubs.

www.bluffdalevacationfarm.com 217-983-2854

•

A roof of 200-plus solar panels gleams at the **Kohl Children's Museum of Greater Chicago**, 2100 Patriot Boulevard, Glenview, which earned a LEED silver award. Outside, the two-acre enclosed Habitat Park encourages a connection to nature through a sensory garden, wind turbine, prairie grass maze and other features. Nine pieces of outdoor sculpture

Get a bug's eye view of colorful plants at Kohl Children's Museum.

encourage interaction, including a kaleidoscope that focuses on colorful plants.

www.kohlchildrensmuseum.org
847-832-6600

•

In 2010, historic preservationists purchased and renovated the **B. Harley Bradley House**, 701 S. Harrison Avenue, Kankakee. Designed in 1900, this was Frank Lloyd Wright's first Prairie-style house. It is open for one-hour tours.

www.kankakeewright.org
815-936-9630

•

Twenty miles southeast of Murphysboro, **Giant City State Park Lodge**, 460 Giant City Lodge Road, Makanda, stands as a long-lasting tribute to indigenous materials. The Civilian Conservation Corps used white oak timber and sandstone to erect the sturdy structure. It was built on the highest point of the park in the 1930s.

Look for the heavy wooden doors, thick hand-hewn beams and a circular stairway that leads to a balcony with nooks for relaxing. Many of the durable, rustic furnishings have withstood the passage of time. The lodge restaurant is known for its fried chicken. Comfortable cabins are just outside the door.

The 4,000-acre park is heavily wooded and rich with hiking and rock climbing on enormous sandstone outcroppings. It is in the 280,000-acre Shawnee National Forest.

www.giantcitylodge.com
618-457-4921

•

The first hotel in Illinois to achieve LEED certification was **Hotel Arista**, 2139 CityGate Lane, Naperville, which earned the distinction in 2009. Smart design means the property uses 30 percent less water and 21 percent less energy than hotels of comparable size. Check out the "nosh box" of regional and organic snacks in the guest rooms. An on-site garden provides some of the ingredients for SugarToad, the hotel restaurant.

www.hotelarista.com 630-579-4100

•

Children's Discovery Museum, 101 E. Beaufort Street, Normal, was the nation's first children's museum to earn a silver level of LEED certification. Exhibits include "Oh Rubbish," where a walk-through landfill talks to visitors. Other activities teach recycling and composting principles.

www.childrensdiscoverymuseum.net 309-433-3444

•

Oberweis Dairy, 951 Ice Cream Drive, North Aurora, is a family business that began with daily home delivery of milk to neighbors in 1927. No synthetic hormones are used in the cattle, and milk comes in returnable glass bottles. Production tours last 45 minutes and end with free samples of ice cream. Call for tour times and days; nominal fee charged.

www.oberweis.com 630-801-6100

•

The Joliet Army Ammunition Plant, about 60 miles southwest of Chicago, produced a billion pounds of TNT and 926 million bombs, shells and other weaponry during World War II on its nearly 37,000 acres. By the time this federal enterprise was deemed inactive in 1993, it occupied 23,500 acres. Now most of the property has been transformed into **Midewin National Tallgrass Prairie**. Environmental cleanup continues, an educational center is planned and one-third of the land (with miles of recreational trails) already is open to the public. It's the largest green space in the Chicago metro area. Get acquainted at the visitor center, 30239 Highway 53, Wilmington, Illinois.

www.fs.fed.us/mntp 815-423-6370

Hike in the 4,000-acre Giant City State Park, part of the Shawnee National Forest (page 26).

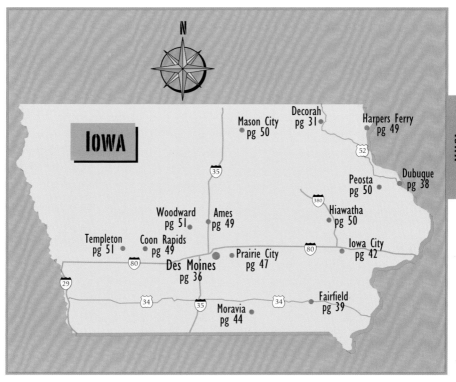

Mason City
pg 50

Decorah
pg 31

Harpers Ferry
pg 49

52

IOWA

35

Peosta
pg 50

Dubuque
pg 38

380

Woodward
pg 51

Ames
pg 49

Hiawatha
pg 50

Templeton
pg 51

Coon Rapids
pg 49

Iowa City
pg 42

80

Prairie City
pg 47

80

Des Moines
pg 36

29

34

35

Moravia
pg 44

34

Fairfield
pg 39

One-of-a-kind projects protect, preserve, promote the land and its inhabitants. A special farm protects the many seeds of our heritage. India-based principles make a huge impact on a small town.

Ride the Ferris wheel and enjoy a bird's-eye view of the Iowa State Fair (page 36).

Return to the simple life, before the electronic age.

FERN HOLLOW CABIN

Decorah, Iowa

Fresh flowers fill a half-dozen containers. Gingersnaps cover a fancy ceramic plate. A jar of mint-flavored water chills in the refrigerator.

I write, doze and consider grabbing a flashlight to sneak a midnight snack from the berry patch, a few steps from the door. Only an owl's occasional hoot interrupts the low but electrifying hum of crickets as darkness thickens.

What I can't do is turn on a TV, hop on the Internet or use a cell phone. Playing a radio is possible, but it would feel like screaming in church. It's so quiet that the flight of a single hummingbird in daylight sounds like a lawn mower run amok.

Booking a stay at the three-room (kitchen, bedroom, sitting room) Fern Hollow Cabin, built in 1853, is one way to live off the grid in northeast Iowa.

Bird chirps are my alarm clock. Ceiling fans do a pretty good job of moving humid air.

Breakfast arrives with a quick knock and a soft song. In a basket, left outside the door, is a note describing its contents: "pecan-currant muffins, yogurt milked and made yesterday, maple syrup from trees you can see out your window, raspberries picked this morning, apple-raspberry juice we made last year, melon from the farmers' market."

The meal appears in a pleasant mismatch of antique and ordinary bottles, jars and linens. I eat at a heavy butcher block table covered with a cross-stitched tablecloth, the kind that fewer and fewer grandmas embroider.

Scavenged handicrafts turn this secluded old house into a home: needlepoint and crochet, quilts and wood carvings, pottery and fine china, a hand-me-down library of books and games. Walking trails cut into a forest. A wooden swing, for two, overlooks a wide garden and wildflowers.

"Built in 1853, revived in 1989," is Liz Rog and Daniel Rotto's description of the log cabin they lived in for 15 years, before renting it to travelers. Liz's great-great-great-grandparents Eivind and Ragnhild Fristad raised six children in two rooms.

Liz and Daniel dismantled the structure, moved it 12 miles and reassembled it on a brick foundation, to add the third room. Two daughters were born and raised in the cabin before the family built a larger house with reclaimed materials, just a few yards away.

Liz says the land and its people, near Decorah, "speak to the deepest part of my soul." She was raised in a Twin Cities suburb and freelances as a musician. Daniel co-owns a taxi service.

They follow a Great Depression mantra: Use it up, wear it out, make it do or do without.

Solar panels provide all electricity. There is no well for water; whatever is used is purchased water or collected rainwater.

A Fern Hollow stay might realign your notion of what it means to be a serious steward of the land, or reinforce your desire to conserve energy.

Head to the compost toilet outdoors (it is moved indoors for winter), or use a chamber pot in the bedroom (but you're responsible for emptying it later). Only cold water runs from the kitchen tap, so boil what you need for cooking and cleaning. To bathe, pour heated water into a bucket next to the shower stall, then switch on the pump to make water spurt from the shower nozzle.

The cost to stay overnight can be bartered down with merchandise or labor. The cabin has one bed and a pull-out sleeper. Children are welcome.

A Fern Hollow neighbor is the **Pepperfield Project**, 1575 Manawa Trail Road, a nonprofit effort that is devoted to rural life skills, including cooking, food preservation and gardening. Co-founder David Cavagnaro is former gardens manager of Seed Savers Exchange. For more about classes: www.pepperfieldproject.org 563-382-8833.

Fern Hollow Cabin
1591 Manawa Trail Road
Decorah, Iowa
www.fernhollowcabin.com 563-382-8013

•

Also in the rural neighborhood:

Waterloo Workshop, 369 Waterloo Creek Drive, Dorchester, where basket weaving, wood carving and food preservation are done by Jill and Michael Stephenson in a log building that has no electricity or telephone.

Drop-ins are welcome, especially from 11 a.m. to 4 p.m. on the second Sunday of every month, when visitors "share fresh, made-from scratch rolls baked in our wood stove, sample country jams and sip tea or fresh well water."

Breakfast is delivered to your cabin door at Fern Hollow.

Gardens waiting to happen at Seed Savers

SEED SAVERS EXCHANGE

Decorah, Iowa

Lovers of heirloom-seed gardening make a pilgrimage to Seed Savers Exchange in northeast Iowa. As on-site educator Devin Parker explains, it's "a mecca for people who are seriously curious about food, beyond what we see in the grocery store."

The 890-acre heritage farm has many demonstration and display gardens that preserve thousands of rare flowers, vegetables, fruits and herbs. About 25,000 types of seeds make up the nonprofit Seed Savers collection.

The work began in 1975 with the seeds from two plants—the German Pink Tomato and Grandpa Ott's Morning Glory—brought to the United States from Bavaria in the 1870s. Diane Ott Whealy, a Seed Savers co-founder, received the seeds from her terminally ill grandfather.

Members of her international organization support the genetic preservation work on the farm's certified-organic property. About 700 of the 1,300 members agree to exchange family heirloom seeds with other members.

The farm's garden for children aims to explain food origins in fun ways, by grouping plants by nation of origin. The preservation gardens show heirloom species in various sizes and shapes of garden plots. In the Historic Orchard are 700 of the estimated 8,000 varieties of apples in existence in 1900; the others are extinct.

An Ark of Taste garden showcases a few of the foods deemed endangered by Slow Food USA. "Edible Asian Garden" is the theme of yet another plot. Elsewhere is a garden that demonstrates how much food can be produced in 100 square feet (the idea came from garden writer Ros Creasy, whose California garden generated $683 in produce after a $36 investment).

The gardens are a living catalog, according to Devin. About 600 of the 25,000 types of heirloom seeds are sold commercially; about 1,000 varieties are available through Seed Savers membership.

Heirloom breeds of poultry and White Park cattle (on British Isles at least since the twelfth century) also are raised on the campus. The fruits (and vegetables) of labor at Seed Savers go to a local school.

Some gardens are two miles apart, to prevent plant cross-pollination. Miles of hiking paths cross the farm but some gardens are scattered and not easily accessible to visitors.

Tours can be arranged. The visitors' center, which includes a retail shop, is open from April through October.

Seed Savers Exchange
3094 N. Winn Road
Decorah, Iowa
www.seedsavers.org 563-382-5990
•

Corn dogs and corn-fed hogs, egg rolling and egg layers compete for prizes.

IOWA STATE FAIR

Des Moines, Iowa

The Iowa State Fair has epitomized Midwest sensibilities, character and cuisine since 1854. Corn-fed, considerate, country-proud and kitchen-savvy. That's the message enthusiastically and unapologetically repeated.

Think "sense of place" and "pride of place."

Much ado stems from big and bizarre contests: beard growing and wood chopping, rubber chicken throwing and weed identifying, horseshoe pitching and marble shooting. Iowa's largest tourism event presents obstacle courses for goats, limbo contests for llamas, agility demos for dogs—plus chicken, duck, rooster and turkey calling contests for people. Pigeons are raced, rolled and auctioned. The lightest and heaviest also earn prizes. Add grape stomps, bull riding, chicken washing, egg rolling, cowboy queens and 60,000 entries in art categories (making this the state's biggest art show).

A new state fair cookbook is printed every other year because cooks can compete in almost 900 ways, sometimes with 50 new categories per year (for example, corncob syrup creations, best corn casserole). Judging begins days before the fair opens. There is no limit on the number of categories that a person can enter, and stakes sometimes are high, as in $3,000 for the top cinnamon roll.

OK, this level of reward is an extreme, but the generosity of food manufacturers and other prize sponsors elevates entry quality and participation in many other categories: $500 for the best old-fashioned fudge, $250 for the top soy recipe, $150 for best "potluck pleaser," $150 for best shortcake.

What else? Among the 50-plus foods on a stick are regional specialties, like the Fudge Puppy (a waffle, covered with chocolate syrup and dabbed with whipped cream) and Chicken Lips (breaded chicken, doused with hot sauce).

Small-town vendors—such as the Wooden Shoe booth, from Pella, population 10,000—find a place here, too. Sticks skewer Dutch Letters (buttery, S-shaped pastries filled with almond paste) from Vander Ploeg Bakery, slabs of ring bologna from Pella's International Veld Meat Market.

Top "fan favorite," as decided by a vote of fair patrons, is the Steer 'N' Stein, on the fairgrounds since 1945 and specializing in a gooey rarebit (a burger and fries covered with spicy cheese sauce).

Just about any celebration of rural living is a good thing, but the Iowa State Fair is what Phil Stong had in mind when writing his 1932 novel, *State Fair*, which inspired three films and a Rodgers and Hammerstein musical of the same name.

The 1885 fairgrounds, a former farmstead, earns a spot on the National Register of Historic Places for its well-preserved art deco and exposition architecture. Competitive hog calling has gone on since 1926. Fiddler contests began in 1925. Big-as-life cows have been sculpted since 1911 (from lard, in the fair's earliest years, from 600 pounds of butter today).

It's all an indication of how seriously Iowans embrace their traditions, their ag products and their annual August homecoming—the state fair.

One definition of ecotourism is that which conserves the environment and improves the well-being of local people. The Iowa State Fair does this and more by protecting, celebrating and promoting its rural heritage in a big way.

Iowa State Fair
East Thirtieth Street and East University Avenue
Des Moines, Iowa
www.iowastatefair.org 800-545-FAIR
•

IOWA

NATIONAL MISSISSIPPI RIVER MUSEUM AND AQUARIUM

Dubuque, Iowa

When the National Mississippi River Museum and Aquarium opened in 2003, it was part of a $188 million riverfront redevelopment project. The facility takes a comprehensive, fun and personal look at the river's history, inhabitants and impact.

It is heavy on the memorabilia of Samuel Clemens, the author better known as Mark Twain. River artwork includes cityscapes from the mid-1800s and pastels from the 1980s. Bios of the 50-plus people in the National Rivers Hall of Fame, such as Meriwether Lewis and Louis Armstrong, are as diverse as the river's residents. River creatures, from barking tree frogs to needle-nosed paddlefish, can be viewed in tanks and, in some cases, touched.

A simulator helps visitors feel what it's like to steer a barge. A huge map of the United States shows major rivers, but no state boundaries. Engaging films drive home the Mississippi's power to give, take and be sapped of life.

National Mississippi River Museum and Aquarium
350 E. Third Street
Dubuque, Iowa
www.mississippirivermuseum.com 800-226-3369
•

Other parts of Dubuque's engaging riverfront are a riverwalk, outdoor amphitheater, events center, lodging, dining and entertainment venues.
www.americasriver.com 800-798-8844

Peace, contemplation and detoxification await you at the Raj.

FAIRFIELD, IOWA

I dunk a wedge of focaccia into the day's soup—Bogota Potato, spiced with a mild curry—at Revelations Cafe and Bookstore, while assessing the pulse of this unusual community in the cornfields of southeast Iowa.

People behind me are talking about energy fields. Another table debates academic freedom versus accreditation. Shelves for used books are categorized as spirituality, Judaism, prayer, reflexology, yoga, herbs.

A table card advertises smoothies spiked with dietary supplements that purport to cleanse the body of impurities and assist with weight loss.

The Ayurveda system of health care is based upon 5,000-year-old principles that originated in India. It involves lifestyle choices that Fairfield, population 9,500, appears to embrace.

References to health, wellness and Ayurvedic products pop up on signs and storefronts throughout Fairfield's town square. The businesses face a tidy gazebo, in a park where yoga classes meet on summery Saturday mornings. Fairfield has jewelry shops, clothing boutiques, health product shops and ethnic eateries.

Abundance EcoVillage, a subdivision, is dedicated to energy and natural resource conservation (through wind and solar power, harvested rainwater, Earth Tube technology for ventilation and other like-minded efforts). Among the first dozen houses is Sweetwater Luxury Bunkhouse, four bedrooms of off-the-grid lodging for travelers.

Fairfield's Go Green plan—fueled by an $80,000 state grant to collect data, create a sustainability guide and hire a program coordinator—aims to make the community a nationwide model of sustainability by 2020.

What inspires these projects and gives the area a global reputation? Look just outside the city limits, to the Maharishi University of Management, open since 1971 and now offering a four-year bachelor's degree in sustainable living.

The school led to establishment of Maharishi Vedic City, where about 1,000 people live in a systematic manner and as a part of the Global Country of World Peace, which pursues a loftier goal: to unite all nations through ancient Vedic principles that include TM, transcendental meditation. All house entrances face the east. Gardens contain no synthetic pesticides or fertilizers. Large-group meditation happens twice daily.

TM also is at the core of business and spirit at the Raj, a medical spa that aims to rid patients of environmental toxins and enhance mind-body connections. Numerous publications—including the *New York Times*, *Los Angeles Times* and various spa magazines—have published positive reviews.

Customers arrive from all continents and include filmmaker David Lynch, rockers Donovan and Mike Love of the Beach Boys. A one-week detox program costs about $4,750, but some stay longer or spend $595 for just one day of treatments, classes and lectures. An initial consultation is $150.

Pulse diagnosis reveals levels and locations of toxins, blockages and digestive and metabolic weaknesses. These factors, body type and basic Vedic rules (such as rise early, exercise in the morning, be in bed early and make lunch your biggest meal) dictate the course of individualized treatment.

"We are not a luxury spa—we don't have a swimming pool here," notes Graciella Zogbi, on-staff Vedic health educator and music therapist. She says the program allows "profound detoxification, rejuvenation and balance" when following "the same authentic Ayurvedic treatments used on the royalty of ancient Vedic India."

This involves oil enemas, vegetarian meals, no alcohol or drugs and 2.5 hours of daily spa services, such as massage, light beam therapy, trickling herb-infused oil onto the forehead, detoxing from shoulders to feet in a chamber of steam.

Some patients yearn to ward off the effects of aging. Others fight the pain of fibroids or infertility. The Raj makes no guarantees but suggests that any condition, from allergy to ulcers, can improve or vanish, when accompanied by permanent lifestyle and diet changes.

Graciella believes perfect health is a matter of choice and, similarly, "if you want societal peace, you start with individual peace" of mind through TM, "which helps us naturally and spontaneously want to do good things for our body."

Curious visitors are welcome to pick up a self-guided tour handout or make a reservation for lunch (a vegetarian buffet) at the spa's restaurant.

For more about the Raj, 1734 Jasmine Avenue, Fairfield: www.theraj.com, 800-248-9050.

Fairfield Iowa Convention and Visitors Bureau
200 N. Main Street
Fairfield, Iowa
www.travelfairfieldiowa.com 641-472-2828
•

An up-to-the-minute menu lets you know what's fresh at Devotay.

DEVOTAY

Iowa City, Iowa

The potter and the chef are good listeners with an entrepreneurial spirit. They like to tinker and please.

That's why the spice blends and infused oils that they developed for themselves ended up at Iowa City's farmers' market. Then they'd stage demos at the market, to show how the products could be used with items purchased from other vendors.

That led to a storefront for a product line that also included hot sauces and jams, named Devotay (after their son, Devon, and daughter, Taylor). Then came catering, and the present restaurant. Kurt Michael and Kim Friese have since led their community in all sorts of other ways.

They organize workshops for restaurateurs, about how to work with local farmers. It works the other way, too. Good communication and clear expectations are important when dealing with people too busy with work to waste time, and that's one thing farmers and chefs have in common.

The couple also publish *Edible Iowa River Valley*, a quarterly magazine that celebrates the use of locally produced food. Kurt advocates the message nationally, as a board member for Slow Food USA and as author of *A Cook's Journey: Slow Food in the Heartland*.

"He's the creative one, and I'm the practical one," says Kim. Their interest in using local ingredients began as more about logic than sentiment, while Kurt was a student at the New England Culinary Institute.

"For him, it was more about flavor—'fresh' ingredients meant better flavor," Kim explains, so making down-the-road purchases made sense. They began working with one local farmer, Simon Delaty, a retired French professor who raised goats, made cheese and baked fougasse (a flatbread, similar to focaccia) in a wood-fired oven.

Today about 40 vendors work with Devotay, and each is paid on delivery for what they sell. "It may sound dangerous as a business model, but all is well accounted for," Kim says.

They also buy from a CSA, whose weekly surprises "make it interesting for the chefs and give them a creative outlet."

Menus change seasonally, weighing clientele expectations against local product availability. "We'd never take the chicken salad off the lunch menu," Kim says. The paella is similarly popular for dinner.

"Our mission is local, but our theme is Spanish," she says, because of a Mediterranean influence of flavors. The couple's decision to establish a tapas menu was a dining concept new for the area and practical. They were "the only employees and could do the prep work during the day, then serve easily."

All meats, year-round, come from within 100 miles of Iowa City. "We buy direct from the farmers," Kim says. She knows it's hard for restaurants to break into the buy-local model, "but if you can buy even one or two things, it makes a difference." It's the same for the average consumer, she believes, but those who try "soon realize it's fun."

Devotay
117 N. Linn Street
Iowa City, Iowa
www.devotay.net 319-354-1001
•

Honey Creek offers several lodging options.

HONEY CREEK RESORT STATE PARK

Moravia, Iowa

"Iowa is a tourist export state," the 1974 newspaper article explained, "primarily because it does not have the facilities and attractions to either bring out-of-state travelers or keep Iowans in Iowa."

Ouch.

The Iowegian and Citizen, Centerville, argued for a government-owned, 800-acre resort, about 25 miles from the Iowa-Missouri border. Its lodge "would bring a new quality of life to Iowa," declared the newspaper, describing the project as "more than just an idle dream."

That was 1974, and it took more than 30 years of politics and planning before the doors to Honey Creek Resort opened. "The torch changed hands several times, but the dream stayed alive," says Andy Woodrick, general manager.

But the result is a lodge with 105 guest rooms, 28 cottages (one to four bedrooms), an 18-hole golf course, indoor waterpark, RV park and convention center on the state's biggest tract of prairie (which extends to the lodge's front door). Modern amenities include plasma-screen TVs, free Internet access and hotel-level plushness in furnishings.

"What we have is top-notch lodging, but also an easy way for people to connect with nature and wildlife," Andy says.

"Park lodging" doesn't mean rustic. Dozens of environmentally friendly practices demonstrate Honey Creek's zeal for commitment to sustainability: geothermal heating/cooling, a playground of recycled materials, preferential parking for hybrid vehicles, Iowa products on menus. LEED certification is imminent; it's just a question of what level. It's the same for Audubon International golf course certification.

The park's activity and interpretive center is Interlock House, a solar structure designed and built by Iowa State University students. The building produced more energy than it consumed during a solar decathlon in Washington, D.C.

Andy says organized activities for children, such as naturalist talks and sandcastle building, are commonplace because "couples take care of themselves and conventions have their own agendas, but we have to make sure families have enough to do." Narrated boat rides at twilight and beginner kayaking classes also engage adults.

The resort's Lake Rathbun was established in 1969, the result of a flood control project, and is Iowa's largest lake.

Honey Creek Resort State Park
12633 Resort Drive
Moravia, Iowa
www.honeycreekresort.com 877-677-3344
•

The lodge at Honey Creek (page 44) is not your typical state park lodge.

Thousands of acres of tallgrass prairie are home to wild bison and meadowlarks.

NEAL SMITH
NATIONAL WILDLIFE REFUGE
Prairie City, Iowa

Up to 70 million bison long roamed North America on 140 million acres of tallgrass prairie. Unregulated greed, whims and ambition decimated the population and its habitat during the 1800s.

We plowed under and built over the land. We slaughtered the animals for meat, hides and sport.

Less than 4 percent of the tallgrass prairie remains. Only about 500 bison were alive by the time a federal law in 1894 was enacted to protect the species. Today about 200,000 wild bison roam the plains, and that includes a herd on more than 5,300 acres of central Iowa.

A meadowlark proclaims his territory.

The Neal Smith refuge, established in 1991 and named after a former congressman, reconstructs the environment that existed before European immigrants settled the area in the 1840s. This means reintroduction of oak savanna as well as tallgrass prairie, a herd of elk as well as bison and many other plant and creature communities.

The project is considered the nation's largest reconstruction of a tallgrass prairie ecosystem. Consider native prairie flowers and grasses. More than 200 types thrive here.

A goal is to acquire up to 8,654 acres for restoration. Visit the Prairie Learning Center at the refuge, to better understand the history, work and dynamics of the endeavor.

Drive through the area's 1,000-acre wildlife enclosure, for a glimpse of the home where the bison now roam. Or walk five miles of paved and blacktop trails to better appreciate the area's other inhabitants.

It's not all about massive-sized mammals. Meadowlarks and monarch butterflies live here, too.

Neal Smith National Wildlife Refuge
9981 Pacific Street
Prairie City, Iowa
www.fws.gov/midwest/NealSmith 515-994-3400

•

MORE GREEN PLACES TO VISIT

Reiman Gardens, 1407 University Boulevard, Ames, is an Iowa State University property that demonstrates a fervent interest in sustainability. Reiman Gardens also is known for its gnomes, which are good luck charms, and has more than 50, including the world's largest (15 feet tall), made from concrete (3,500 pounds).

www.reimangardens.iastate.edu 515-294-2710

•

At the core of 4,300-acre **Whiterock Conservancy**, 1390 Highway 141, Coon Rapids, is a bed-and-breakfast that was the home of Roswell Garst, a farmer who helped create hybrid seed corn and in 1959 hosted a visit by Soviet leader Nikita Khrushchev. Artifacts from that historic cold war event are on display. Cottages are another lodging option.

www.whiterockconservancy.org 712-684-2697

•

Our Lady of the Mississippi Abbey, 8400 Abbey Hill Lane, Dubuque, is a community of Trappist nuns who follow the Benedictine way of life.

Guests stay in one of two houses on the grounds, or a two-room hermitage, a homelike lodging, without TVs or radios.

The nuns produce about 70,000 pounds of caramel candy annually in an environmentally thoughtful, geothermal facility. Chocolates and caramels are boxed and shipped throughout the country. They also are sold at a small gift shop at the abbey.

This is a cloistered community, that is, most of the nuns do not interact with the public. They made an exception for five women to stay at the monastery for 40 days and experience the Benedictine life for a reality TV series that aired on the Learning Channel.

www.mississippiabbey.org 563-582-2595
www.monasterycandy.com 866-556-3400

•

Effigy Mounds National Monument, 151 Highway 76, Harpers Ferry, preserves more than 200 prehistoric mounds, 31 of which are in the shape of animals (bear, eagle, turtle, fish) and near the Mississippi River. Prehistoric cultures built an estimated 10,000 mounds in northeast Iowa, but less than one-fourth remain.

www.nps.gov/efmo 563-873-3491

•

IOWA

Two hermitages are available for overnight stays at **Prairiewoods Franciscan Spirituality Center**, 120 E. Boyson Road, Hiawatha. The religious community established these 70 acres as a "shelter for wildlife and natural flora as well as spaces of solitude and peace for those seeking a spiritual connection with the land."

www.prairiewoods.org 319-395-6700

Follow a quiet trail at Effigy Mounds (page 49).

•

The historic **Park Inn Hotel**, 107 E. State Street, Mason City, had been vacant since 1910. Renovation and restoration of the world's last Wright-designed hotel ended in 2011, when the prototype for the Imperial Hotel in Tokyo opened as a boutique hotel. Many of the building's original features were lost or removed as it morphed from hotel to rental apartments.

www.wrightonthepark.org
641-423-0689

•

About 12 miles southwest of Dubuque, Catholic monks not only farm but also craft things from wood, including simple caskets made from the walnut, oak and pine trees in their own sustainable forest. Their Trappist monastery, **New Melleray Abbey**, 6632 Melleray Circle, Peosta, has existed since 1849 and follows the Rule of Benedict.

The stone worship sanctuary is narrow, loft-like and full of natural light. Its 40 arched windows loom above those who gather here, but the area lacks stained glass and religious statues. The plain altar is made of wood; a wrought iron railing separates visitors from monastic residents.

Across the hall is a gift shop that sells jewelry, books, religious icons, pottery, jams, soaps and other products of the community. Even locally grown garlic is sold (four kinds, when I visited).

Overnight guests are welcome, but the 16 small bedrooms fill fast. Each has bathroom facilities. Décor is stark, there is no TV or radio, and silence is encouraged.

www.newmelleray.org 563-588-2319
www.trappistcaskets.com 888-433-6934
•

During Prohibition, Iowans passed around the recipe for Templeton Rye, then quietly put together jugs of the whiskey and sold them (or drank them) to survive the Great Depression. So the product has a longstanding history in Templeton, population 350. Now the hootch is distilled legally by a small company called **Templeton Rye**, 209 E. Third Street, Templeton. A Rock and Rye music fest draws a crowd in August. Free distillery tours are scheduled.

www.templetonrye.com 712-669-8793
•

Eighty Jersey cows and eighty acres. That's the basis for business at the Jeff Burkhart family's **Picket Fence Creamery**, 14583 S Avenue, Woodward. Its monthly Sample Sundays are easy ways to introduce yourself to products from this farm and those of about ninety other families. The farm store sells Iowa wines, elk sticks, bison summer sausage and much more, in addition to Picket Fence meats and dairy products.

www.picketfencecreamery.net 515-438-COWS

*An old insane asylum in Traverse City, Michigan,
has found a new life as Grand Traverse Commons (page 76).*

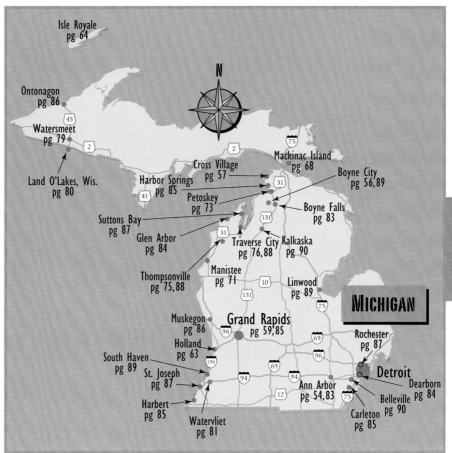

Isle Royale
pg 64

Ontonagon
pg 86

Watersmeet
pg 79

Land O'Lakes, Wis.
pg 80

Harbor Springs
pg 85

Cross Village
pg 57

Mackinac Island
pg 68

Boyne City
pg 56,89

Petoskey
pg 73

Boyne Falls
pg 83

Suttons Bay
pg 87

Glen Arbor
pg 84

Traverse City
pg 76,88

Kalkaska
pg 90

Thompsonville
pg 75,88

Manistee
pg 71

Linwood
pg 89

Muskegon
pg 86

Grand Rapids
pg 59,85

Rochester
pg 87

Holland
pg 63

South Haven
pg 89

St. Joseph
pg 87

Ann Arbor
pg 54,83

Detroit

Dearborn

Harbert
pg 85

Belleville pg 84

Watervliet
pg 81

Carleton pg 85

MICHIGAN

MICHIGAN

Recycle, reclaim, reinvent, reinvest. A specialty products company champions the fruits of local labor. Outdoor sculptures blend into the landscape, near ski slopes.

monday
cornman farms
grass-fed or
a niman ranch burger
with your choice of
all-american cheeses,
served with fries
& salad.
$13.95/ea.

this week's
winner as chosen
by chef alex,
served with a garden
salad & traditional
spider cake.
$13.95/ea.

roadhouse burger

chili cook-off

If you go away hungry from Zingerman's, it's your own fault.

ZINGERMAN'S ROADHOUSE

Ann Arbor, Michigan

He's up at 6 a.m., tending to the tomato crop by 6:30, coaching a work crew about fences for new livestock at 7, beginning the eight-mile drive to his restaurant an hour later. No day is typical for chef Alex Young, but this is his life when we meet on a Saturday morning in late summer. He has forgotten about our interview, for good reason: too much going on.

Alex, the managing partner of Zingerman's Roadhouse, has been a finalist for a James Beard award (best chef, Great Lakes) for four consecutive years. His garden plot is a farm with some 130 varieties of dozens of vegetables, plus an assortment of high-protein tenants with hooves.

The Roadhouse is one leg of the Zingerman food empire, which began with a downtown Ann Arbor deli. Now it includes a bakehouse, creamery, coffee roaster, confectionary, culinary tour company and mail-order business. "We are one company, but each part operates independently," Alex says.

Zingerman's cheeses and bakery goods show up at the restaurant and deli. Cooking and cheese-making classes complement food sales. Food waste ends up as farm compost, whey from cheese production feeds the pigs. Some of Alex's restaurant employees also work on the farm. All make the use of local ingredients a priority.

Customers sit in their cars a half-hour before opening time, to avoid waiting an hour for a table. The impatient approach the Roadshow, a shiny trailer with a to-go menu for people too harried to get out of their car.

"Really good American food" is how the Roadhouse is described. Sweet potato fries are twice-cooked and served with a spicy mayo. The Reuben is dressed with swiss cheese, russian dressing and "hot slaw." That's not to be confused with the pork barbecue, which comes with "mustard cole slaw."

Zingerman's Roadhouse is easy to find: Just look for a bright burst of neon script at Maple Village Shopping Center, a quick shot off of I-94 at Jackson Avenue.

For more about other facets of the Ann Arbor business: www.zingermans.com 888-636-8162. Zingerman's Deli is at 422 Detroit Street in Ann Arbor. www.zingermansdeli.com 734-663-3354

Zingerman's Roadhouse
2501 Jackson Avenue
Ann Arbor, Michigan
www.zingermansroadhouse.com 734-663-3663
•

LAVENDER HILL FARM

Boyne City, Michigan

Linda and Roy Longworth are beekeepers who planted lavender as food for the insects and then became aware of its greater potential. They visited lavender farms in other countries before starting their own business. They saw how lavender thrived along the forty-fifth parallel in both the northern and southern hemispheres. Indigenous limestone deposits in their part of Michigan further enhance the soil conditions for growing it.

Now they have about two dozen types of lavender, grown chemically free, and a farmstead shop that sells many types of lavender products. As a food ingredient, it goes into shortbread, jelly, lemonade, tea, ice cream and marinades. It has uses as a room freshener, skin soother and jet lag reducer. It can help ease the sting of insect bites or relax the mind. The big seller is a spot and stain remover, sold in 12-ounce blocks or a smaller size that fits into a nifty embroidered drawstring bag.

The business employs field workers and sewers of sachets. Lavender fields are at their peak of color between mid-July and mid-August.

Lavender Hill Farm
07354 Horton Bay Road
Boyne City, Michigan
www.lavenderhillmichigan.com 231-582-3784
•

Stove legs make up the second floor railing, thus the name.

LEGS INN

Cross Village, Michigan

Legs Inn is a Polish restaurant built in the 1920s by an immigrant smitten with the natural beauty and Native American influences in the area. Ottawa and Chippewa ties figure prominently in the design.

Stanley Smolak used stones smoothed by lake waves, unusual tree growths and twisted roots to build an extraordinarily distinctive place to sell Native American handiwork and souvenirs. Then he added a tavern and dining room, which have panoramic views of Lake Michigan and are warmed by four stone fireplaces.

Cross Village, population 300, is among the state's oldest settlements and a place where almost two dozen Native American tribes gathered around tribal fires in the late 1700s. The tribes referred to the area as Land of the Cross, for the large white cross that explorer Jacques Marquette erected on a lakeside bluff.

"Legs" is a reference to the stove legs that Stanley used to make a railing on the roof. The business remains family operated, serving *kabanosy* (Polish sausage), *pierogi* (filled dumplings), *bigos* (hunter's stew) and *cwikla* (beet relish). Smoked whitefish spread also is a specialty.

It's a beautiful drive to this small town on Highway 119, and just south is a scenic heritage route, the Tunnel of Trees. Prepare to be wowed. Open May to October.

Legs Inn
6425 N. Lake Shore Drive
Cross Village, Michigan
www.legsinn.com 231-526-2281
•

The perfect place to drink in the view at Legs Inn

Play with the art and cool off too, at Millennium Park, Grand Rapids.

GRAND RAPIDS, MICHIGAN

Grand Rapids is painting its city deep, deep green.

No other metro area, per capita, has more square footage that meets LEED standards, announced the U.S. Green Building Council in 2008.

The area also has one of the world's highest concentrations of environmentally progressive buildings and earned the title of "America's greenest city" from *Fast Company* magazine.

The momentum continues and seems contagious in Grand Rapids. The Green Chauffeur taxis people around town in a hybrid Toyota Prius. Ellen Markel, general manager of the downtown Holiday Inn, offers local residents no-fee recycling of Christmas trees.

People call Patricia Pennell the "queen of rain gardens" because she snagged the www.raingardens.org address for her employer, the West Michigan Environmental Action Council. Today she fields questions about rain gardens from as far away as India.

The area's most excessively ambitious goal is LEED certification of Grand Valley State University's entire Allendale campus, in suburban Grand Rapids. Eleven campus buildings already are certified.

Then there are LEED projects of interest to the average tourist.

The **Grand Rapids Art Museum** in 2008 was the nation's first art museum to achieve a gold level of LEED certification. Rainwater collected in an underground cistern helps to water lawns and wash dishes. A reflecting pool becomes a winter skating rink. Skylights in galleries and other sources of filtered but natural lighting lessen the need for artificial light. This element was not an easy feat: Too much exposure to sunshine tends to damage artwork.

The new $75 million museum building was anchored with $20 million from the foundation of local philanthropist and environmentalist Peter Wege. The museum's permanent collection ranges from Renaissance to modern art. It is downtown at 101 Monroe Center. More at www.artmuseumgr.org, 616-831-1000.

Also in Grand Rapids is Michigan's first LEED restaurant, the **Green Well**, a classy-casual eatery that earns silver certification. The business features locally made furniture, locally produced artwork and reclaimed local materials. The cherrywood bar top comes from a tree that fell onto the owner's property. Fake slate (recycled plastic) tops patio tables outdoors.

The menu favors locally grown food when convenient. A specialty is mac and cheese: corkscrew pasta with a four-cheese sauce, ham, bacon, caramelized onions and other veggies. The restaurant is at 924 Cherry Street, in the city's Uptown district. More at www.thegreenwell.com, 616-808-3566.

Long-term projects include **Millennium Park**, 1,500 acres of former gravel and sand pits that are being converted into a recreational area that is twice the size of Manhattan's Central Park.

"We're taking an [environmentally] exhausted area and reclaiming it," says Roger Sabine, landscape architect.

The 20-year project involves multiple property owners, mining operations and municipalities. The Grand River runs through the area and eventually will feed 14 little lakes that are linked as one, for canoeing or kayaking. These former mining pits are 4 to 28 feet deep.

Already finished is a sandy beach, boathouse, "splash bed" play area, playground and fishing area, at a cost of $25 million. Work proceeds on 20 miles of hiking and biking trails, a $5 million network.

Will the project be LEED certified? "That's the goal," says Roger. It will depend on the willingness of municipal governments and private donors to fund work at this level. A higher investment upfront is typical with LEED projects; payback comes when energy efficiency brings lower operational and maintenance costs.

On the drawing board are plans for a 12,000-seat amphitheater, a visitor center and nature/sustainability center.

The park is at 1415 Maynard Avenue, off of Highway 196, between John Ball Zoo and Johnson Park. **More at www.millennium-park.org.**

*Eat well at the Green Well, Michigan's
first LEED-certified restaurant.*

CityFlats Hotel

Holland, Michigan

Every guest room has a different look at CityFlats, but all 56 rooms have a couple of things in common. Furniture was designed and built by a local company, Charter House Innovations, and the use of reclaimed or quickly renewable materials (cotton, bamboo) was a priority.

Two dozen seats from a closed IMAX theater furnish a hotel conference room. Guest rooms have bamboo fiber linens and towels. Ceiling to floor windows cut the need for artificial light.

Laminated cork and polished concrete floors replace carpeting. Countertops are IceStone (a mix of recycled glass and concrete) or a blend of concrete and crushed beer bottles. Hallways are Plynyl, a textured tile made of fiberglass and vinyl that looks like fabric but is laid like tile.

The boutique hotel, which opened in 2008, was one of the first U.S. hotels to earn LEED gold certification.

A wood-fired oven and outdoor rooftop seating set the mood at the hotel's fifth-floor restaurant, CityVu Bistro. Flatbread pizzas are a specialty. So is carrot cake, made in mini loaves and served warm, with a side of cream cheese frosting. The wine list earns a Wine Spectator Award of Excellence.

A second CityFlats opened in Grand Rapids, Michigan. The LEED-caliber project revamps a long-vacant building at 83 Monroe Center. Like the mother property, each of the 28 guest rooms has a different color scheme and layout.

CityFlats Hotel
61 E. Seventh Street
Holland, Michigan
www.cityflatshotel.com 866-609-2489

•

(left) CityVu Bistro at CityFlats specializes in flatbread pizza.

MICHIGAN

Gorgeous water and interesting rock formations are abundant.

ISLE ROYALE NATIONAL PARK
Michigan

Our 100-passenger ferry is rocking me like a drunken sailor, so I keep my eyes closed during most of this three-hour ride. Never expect Lake Superior to behave, but putting up with impudence sometimes yields exquisite rewards.

Isle Royale National Park is an archipelago of 400-some islands, the longest of which is 45 miles. Backpackers and kayakers can roam for days and not repeat their route. The world's longest-running predator-prey research project, involving moose and wolves, began here more than 50 years ago.

Day visits to Isle Royale's Rock Harbor are possible but illogical. Why endure the six-hour boat ride, with only two or three hours to explore? Ferries cruise roundtrip daily. Four-person seaplane service from Houghton, Michigan, cuts the trip to the park to 35 minutes but is more expensive than the ferry ride.

"You don't go to Isle Royale unless you're committed to being there," concludes Phyllis Green, superintendent. Her park is one of the least visited in the National Park Service.

Isle Royale gets about as many visitors in a year (16,000) as the Grand Canyon averages on a summer day, but the average Isle Royale stay is four days, compared with about six hours at the Grand Canyon.

One out of four who visit Isle Royale will return another time, and this ratio of repeat business is one of the highest among national parks.

Wild orchids bloom in the summer.

You'll see kayaks and canoes, but not autos, bicycles or pets. Only 17 types of mammals make Isle Royale their home, says ranger Mark Kudrav.

Mosquitoes and black flies irritate in swarms until late July, but Lyme disease and poison ivy are not a problem. Ticks threaten the health of moose but not humans.

Most visitors come to backpack and camp; some will hire a water taxi to take them miles away and then hike back to Rock Harbor. A popular starting point, Chippewa Harbor, is a 12-mile walk. The trek back can be tranquil or arduous, depending upon weather and a hiker's preparedness.

Camping is rustic. A few campsites have three-sided shelters, to screen out insects and wildlife. Bring your own tent and gear for wilderness camping.

The less adventurous bring their own provisions and rent one of 20 roomy housekeeping cottages with kitchenettes. Rock Harbor Lodge accommodates still others in 60 motel rooms; you can add hearty meals to the daily rate. A snack bar cooks up lighter fare; all menus depend on provisions delivered by ferry.

Breathtaking views from Lookout Louise are worth the breathtaking climb.

"Most people find there's more to do than they expected," says Kim Alexander, lodge manager. Park rangers organize hikes and evening talks about the islands' history or habitat.

"The first time you see visitors, they're backpackers," he says. "Then that 50-pound pack gets heavy and they come as lodge guests during their next visit."

A few miles away, at Edisen Island, Leslie Mattson shares his love for commercial fishing with the occasional visitor; he and his wife, Donna, maintain a small home at water's edge. A short hike uphill leads to the park's oldest lighthouse, built in 1855. Head in another direction, and you'll find the headquarters for the predator-prey research.

Excursion boats also take the curious toward Lookout Louise, where on a clear day you'll see Canada. At Hidden Lake, hear the birds sing and watch for moose at the shoreline. Wild orchids and roses dot the landscape in summer.

The waters surrounding Isle Royale have been the site of 10 major shipwrecks. Scuba diving is a popular sport; wetsuits or drysuits are a must in the 45-degree water.

The ferry ride back to Copper Harbor is smooth and beguiling, just the opposite of how this trip began. Lake Superior changes that fast.

The park is open from mid-April to late October. Campsite reservations are not accepted for groups of fewer than seven; it's first-come first-served.

Isle Royale National Park
800 E. Lakeshore Drive
Houghton, Michigan
www.nps.gov/isro 906-482-0984

•

Rock Harbor Lodge, the only motel and cottage accommodations on the island, is open from late May to early September. Reservations are necessary.
www.isleroyaleresort.com 906-337-4993

•

The **Isle Royale Queen IV**'s three-hour ferry rides from Copper Harbor, Michigan, run from mid-May to late September. Ferry service also departs from Houghton, Michigan (a six-hour trip), and Grand Portage, Minnesota (three hours, but to Windigo, which is at the opposite end from Rock Harbor). Reservations are necessary.
www.isleroyale.com 906-289-4437

Rock Harbor scene, Isle Royale

Take a ride back in time.

MACKINAC ISLAND
Michigan

Most people visit Michigan's Mackinac Island for just a few hours, so they're more likely to study fudge shops and fort history than contemporary city rhythms.

Up to 15,000 travelers per summer day roam the island's roads and trails on foot, bicycle, horse or horse-drawn carriage. Motorized vehicles were banned in the 1890s, so about 600 horses work here seasonally. By winter when the people population shrinks to around 500, no more than 20 horses remain.

How appropriate it is to frame Mackinac Island, a National Historic Landmark, as a pretty, quaint and unique nautical community that clings to a bygone era.

The lack of cars is a novelty when you're a tourist. It's a way of life that involves commitment and challenges when you're a year-round islander. "We can't lose the ambiance or historic nature of our island, but we also are a real community and have to keep the balance," says Margaret Doud, mayor of Mackinac Island.

It's a challenge to uphold identity. After a Starbucks opened, a city ordinance was enacted to prohibit chain enterprises. A Tastee Freez and Pizza Hut are island history; neither remains in business. The city hopes to establish historic districts. Some residents worry that developers will demolish old buildings without discernment or discussion.

Police ride bicycles unless an emergency requires a patrol car. Fire, ambulance and utility vehicles are available. The island

Police force transportation at the ready

has a snowplow, and residents operate snowmobiles from November 15 to the end of March. Other than that, it's all about two- and four-legged travel. Rules are firmly enforced; that includes golf carts—don't even think about using one to cross a street without a permit.

Three miles long, two miles wide and eight miles around: That's the size of Mackinac Island, and 25 percent of the waste—about 5,800 tons per year—is horse manure. The job of removing it quickly and discreetly was a Dirty Jobs topic on the Discovery Channel. Add waste from restaurants (the largest hotel serves at least 1,000 guests and staff per meal during the height of summer) and the expense of transporting garbage to a mainland landfill (the island capped its own dumping ground decades ago).

All this means that islanders turned "green" long before it became fashionable. They recycle or pay $3 per bag of landfill waste. In the 1970s, a Nebraska farmer set up an island-wide composting system to turn organic garbage into compost and fertilizer. So now you know why all those flowers look so lush, including the 2,500 Yours Truly geraniums that line the 660-foot-long porch at **Grand Hotel**, the world's largest summer hotel that is family owned.

Grand Hotel, built in 1887 and perched on a bluff, is Mackinac Island's beacon. It's also known for its genteel atmosphere, no-tipping policy and no guest rooms decorated alike. Overnight rates tend to include dinner (where men are required to wear a coat and tie) and breakfast.

The 500,000 gallons of heated water in the pool recirculates in a water-based air-conditioning system that cools the hotel's oldest 170 (out of 385) guest accommodations. It's an example of how islanders work to reduce their carbon footprint.

Mayor Doud operates the **Windermere Hotel**, just steps from the harbor and built as a summer cottage in 1887. The 26 guest rooms of this third-generation family business have private baths but no television. Success, in part, depends upon cooperation among businesses, including competitors. "Our barometer is the Grand Hotel," she says. "The island opens and closes with the Grand's season."

"We both need each other to do well," agrees Bob Tagatz, the Grand's historian.

About 83 percent of the island is Michigan State Parks property, and this includes Fort Mackinac, established during the American Revolution and site of two War of 1812 battles. Many of Mackinac Island's 1,200 rooms, suites and cottages remain open into autumn. Rates drop after Labor Day.

Ferries from St. Ignace and Mackinaw City make multiple daily runs to the island until the end of October, and the ride takes less than 20 minutes. Off-season ferry service runs until the waterway freezes, and there is a small airport.

www.mackinacisland.org 906-847-6418

•

Grand Hotel
286 Grand Avenue
Mackinac Island, Michigan
www.grandhotel.com 800-334-7263

•

Windermere Hotel
7498 Main Street
Mackinac Island, Michigan
www.windermerehotel.com 800-847-3125

DOUGLAS VALLEY VINEYARD ESTATES
Manistee, Michigan

Does it take a village to farm organically on a large scale? Might like-minded people want to live in a community that plants and reaps much of what they eat?

Cliff Boomer aims to make 250 of his 640-acre estate a neighborhood of minifarms.

His Douglas Valley fruit farm dates back to the early 1900s, when trains stopped right next to the huge fruit cellar, one-half of which is underground.

The same family owned a second fruit farm about an hour north, making this among the largest fruit growers in the nation. Today the business needs more arms to make it work, because the acreage is certified organic and thus requires more time to tend.

Consider the crops: 90 acres of apple trees, 30 acres of cherries, 7 acres of blueberry bushes and 13 acres of chardonnay, reisling, pinot noir and pinot gris grape vines. Another 200 acres of grains supply a neighboring farm. An 8-acre organic vegetable garden produces about 30 weekly CSA shares.

The model for an organic farm in the Midwest is more like 40 acres, says Cliff. "The weeding and decision to use no chemicals make for a tremendous challenge."

Visitors come to tour, linger and sip hard ciders and fruit wines. A retail shop (a former worker bunkhouse) sells products from neighboring farms, sometimes through bartering for goods and services. I meet a baker who is renting the estate's commercial kitchen to make bagels and raisin bread. Another entrepreneur uses the kitchen (a former fruit packing house) to press and process fruit into juices.

The land parcels are hilly and picturesque; some offer distant views of Lake Michigan. Part of *Return to the Hiding Place*, a World War II movie, was shot here.

When I met Cliff, he had sold one of the 18 minifarms proposed for the 90 acres in Phase I of his project. He wants purchasers to agree to "plant some-thing—grapes, lavender or whatever fits in with the land" on these 2- to 6-acre plots. "We appeal to people in a transitional phase of life," he believes. "Instead of living next to a golf course, this is a way to be productive."

He envisions a community largely operated by the people who live in it, including a general store, a town center and whatever other services seem vital.

He believes up to 200 units could be built without greatly affecting the fruit crops.

"It's about bringing people back to the farm," Cliff says. "For years and years, there's been a conflict between farms and the houses near them. Here, everybody is a part of the farm."

Douglas Valley Vineyard Estates
5375 Douglas Valley Road
Manistee, Michigan
www.douglasvalley.net 231-887-3333
●

*Douglas Valley aims to become a neighborhood of small farms
that are environmentally friendly.*

American Spoon makes its own preserves from domestic and wild fruits.

AMERICAN SPOON
Petoskey, Michigan

It takes a special person to mess with thimbleberries. The tart fruit is softer than a raspberry and harder to pluck, so the berry is not as easy to harvest or keep pretty when shipping.

Who'd want the hassle? Justin Rashid knows they're worth it.

He used to forage through thimbleberry shrubs as a kid, and by 1980 he was selling wild berries to New York City chefs, including Larry Forgione (the "godfather of American cuisine"). Now Justin takes the best of Michigan's fruits, including thimbleberries, and sells them to the world.

About 85 percent of the ingredients in his American Spoon product line are from Michigan. That includes Michigan sugar, derived from sugar beets.

"Best preserves in America." "Michigan in a jar." "Paris has nothing on Michigan when it comes to jam." These are a few of the accolades that American Spoon has earned.

The business began in the basement of a candy store. "Then we moved upstairs," says Justin, "so people could see us cook and smell what we were doing."

Justin explains that his parents' home was next to 30,000 acres of state-owned land that was rich with wild berries, morel mushrooms, crab apples and "a lot of other wonderful things that people don't want to deal with."

So he developed a connection to the land and its gifts that has grown into an appreciation for fine food locally grown. Red Haven peaches and Early Glow strawberries are among the fruit that American Spoon seeks.

"We pay farmers more than they'd get from a large fruit processor," he says.

The company will pit, peel and process in-season fruits by hand, and this becomes the year-round inventory. Pears, apricots, crab apples, damson plums, cherries, rhubarb and more turn into ten-gallon batches of jams, jellies and salsas. Fifty foragers gather elderberries, blackberries and other fruits of the wild.

"We produce flavors and textures that can't be found anywhere else," Justin says. A newer product is Jammys, intense fruit puree candies that are cooled on marble slabs before being cut into sugary squares. Now the company is developing a currant jelly.

"There are people who will build a company just to flip and sell it," Justin says. "For us, it's a lifestyle, a way to make a living and provide jobs. It's an honor to do what we do, and our products help us celebrate our love for this state."

"Make Your Case," a program that persuades customers to order a case of products and get a shipping discount, is a way to encourage larger orders.

"Even when times are hard, there are certain things that people won't give up," Justin maintains, and he believes his product niche makes it easier for customers to stay loyal.

"These are great times for us," Justin says. "We are celebrating a sense of place and the foods of our area—ideas that were on the fringe when this company was beginning. Now we have a food and agritourism revolution that goes back to our roots."

Look for American Spoon retail outlets in these Michigan cities: Petoskey (also home to the American Spoon cafe), Harbor Springs, Charlevoix, Williamsburg, Traverse City and Saugatuck.

American Spoon Cafe
411 E. Lake Street
Petoskey, Michigan
www.spoon.com 231-347-1739
•

MICHIGAN LEGACY ART PARK
Thompsonville, Michigan

This gallery has no walls, so artwork blends with the natural landscape, changing with shadows and sunlight, rain and snow.

On these thirty acres, mostly forested and adjacent to Mountain Ridge Golf Course, are more than 40 outdoor sculptures that explain and interpret the makings of Michigan. Hikers are in for a treasure hunt as they walk the park's two miles of trails. Borrow a trail guide to learn about the artists' intentions or simply enjoy the sculptural surprises that emerge as you walk.

Look through John Sauve's "Man in His Element," a human form cut out of an eight-foot-tall sheet of steel, and you'll see the golf course's eighteenth hole. "Frog," by Bill Allen, is an amphibian-on-steroids rendition that appears ready to leap.

"Fairy Ring," by David Barr, is a reference to mushrooms that are commonplace in Michigan. He also offers the "Stockade Labyrinth," through which walkers weave their way to a little lookout at the top.

Elsewhere are tributes to white-tailed deer, wheels of progress, old-time logging camps and Ernest Hemingway (who spent summers in northern Michigan and loved fishing there).

Michigan Legacy Art Park
12500 Crystal Mountain Drive
Thompsonville, Michigan
www.michlegacyartpark.org 231-378-4963
•

Bill Allen molded galvanized steel, coated with copper, to create the alert-looking "Frog."

MICHIGAN

During much of the 1900s, this building was devoted to potato peeling.

VILLAGE AT
GRAND TRAVERSE COMMONS
Traverse City, Michigan

Sunshine, fresh air, beauty as therapy, physical exercise through work. These were crucial components of mental health treatment in the mid-1800s, and Dr. Thomas Story Kirkbride of Pennsylvania came up with plans to practice them throughout the United States.

His sturdy insane asylums were zigzag, two-wing buildings full of windows and cross-ventilation, typically with views of uncluttered and serene settings. Farm work and other tasks would attempt to divert those with inner demons.

Administrative offices, in the middle of the asylum, separated male and female patients. The most troubled roomed on the lowest floor and were farthest from the building's center, so their behavior would not interfere with the rehab of others.

Almost all of the nation's estimated 80 Kirkbride developments for natural healing (www.kirkbridebuildings.com) were destroyed when mental health treatment philosophies changed to emphasize in-community care, drug therapy and psychoanalysis. The one in Traverse City, an 1885 structure that is one-quarter mile long and used to house 3,500 mental health patients on 1,100 acres, is an exception. Now Building 50, bit by bit, is being transformed into a residential, retail and public gathering spot—the largest in the area.

"You can't get any greener than rehabbing an old building," says developer Ray Minervini, a Detroit native who moved to Traverse City in the 1980s. "Detroit used to be a beautiful city," he says. "I saw a remarkable number of buildings there destroyed through neglect. Europe cherishes its antiquities, but we don't."

By 1989, the Traverse City asylum had closed and the last 480 acres were sold to the city and township for $1. The first thought was to demolish the empty buildings, but that generated public uproar. Ray didn't like the idea either, and he was part of a panel that solicited and studied alternatives, all of which fell through as the campus continued to deteriorate.

Water had been pouring into the building for years, so Ray proposed re-shingling and made a $1.5 million personal investment. In return, he got ownership of the structures for $1, and now building rehab proceeds as time and money allow.

Bit by bit, this dilapidated building is being brought back to life at Grand Traverse Commons.

Today the asylum's former fire station is a bakery. A building used for potato peeling is a restaurant. A winery (selling by the glass or growler) and coffee roaster occupy the former laundry facility.

On the ground level of Building 50 is the Mercato, an assortment of independently owned boutiques and bistros. Offices fill the first floor and are topped by three floors of condos, many with waterfront views of Traverse Bay.

At the core of development are 64 acres and 7,000 square feet of the main building. The remaining 416 acres is Traverse City's biggest parcel of community gardens and parkland with trails for hiking, bicycling and snowshoeing. The front lawn is the site of farmers' markets, concerts, festivals and weddings.

"I used all resources available to me . . . my retirement fund, hocked my house," Ray says. He mentions the 2-foot-thick brick walls, 2,000 windows and 14-foot ceilings in Building 50, and thinks it was ahead of its time in several ways. He says the asylum had electricity 28 years before the rest of Traverse City. Steam turbines produced electricity and heat through underground tunnels until 1950, when replaced by more conventional systems that are now out of date.

"We'll never build something like this again—it would be too expensive," Ray says. "But you can see why this building will be here 500 to 1,000 years from now."

Condos range from 300-square-foot efficiency units to those with multiple bedrooms. Some are rented by the night, week or month. Some of the building's full-time residents work in the area and refer to their neighbors as the "village people" because of the sense of community that accompanies their living arrangement.

"This costs us at least twice as much as new construction— $200 to $250 per square foot, compared to $100," Ray says. "But we can't continue to build sprawl, and we're beginning to realize that sprawl doesn't work anyway."

Village at Grand Traverse Commons
1200 W. Eleventh Street
Traverse City, Michigan
www.thevillagetc.com 231-941-1900
•

Clear lakes and tall pine trees punctuate the wilderness at Sylvania.

SYLVANIA WILDERNESS

Ottawa National Forest
Watersmeet, Michigan

In the Upper Midwest we all have our own ideas about where the Northwoods begins, but how do you define true wilderness? Is it simply the lack of condo developments? A disappearance of road signs? The suspicion that more critters inhabit an area than people? Many trees, no cows?

True wilderness means much more. Sylvania Wilderness, about 18,300 acres inside of Ottawa National Forest in Michigan, is right where the state abuts Wisconsin's border.

You get a taste of the rugged beauty from the car, but you can see the core only by hiking, canoeing or cross-country skiing on 20 to 25 miles of unmarked trails. Bring a compass, or a GPS, plus a map of the area to find your way.

Sylvania has been U.S. Forest Service property since 1967 and was designated federal wilderness 20 years later. It includes about three dozen pure and undeveloped lakes, plus virgin timbers of pine and hemlock in old-growth forests.

That means the land is preserved in its natural state for the benefit of its inhabitants, not the tourists, who must abide by strict regulations when visiting.

This includes students at Conserve School, a college prep boarding program for gifted students on 1,200 acres, near Land O' Lakes, Wisconsin, and bordering Sylvania Wilderness. An annual exercise in winter survival requires students, on cross-country skis, to figure out how to get from wilderness to school property. It typically is a nine-mile journey.

Sylvania Wilderness exists as it is, in part, because a lumber baron in the late 1800s decided the forest was too beautiful to cut. The land slowly turned into a paradise for the wealthy, but today the local economy seems to struggle because travelers tend to gravitate toward more easily accessible lodging that has modern amenities and diverse dining options.

Not much traffic on this road

Sylvania Wilderness
Ottawa National Forest Visitor Center
Highways 45 and 2
Watersmeet, Michigan
www.fs.fed.us/r9/ottawa
906-358-4724
•

Gateway Lodge, 4103 Highway B, Land O' Lakes, Wisconsin (south of Watersmeet), was built with local timbers in the 1930s. During its heyday, in the 1940s and 1950s, celebrity visitors included Bob Hope, Mitzi Gaynor, Lawrence Welk, Bud Abbott and Lou Costello. President Eisenhower's family fished in the area. Astronaut James Lovell made this his secret retreat.

Adjacent to the lodge is the nine-hole Gateway Golf Course, where the third tee is in Wisconsin but the third fairway is in Michigan. For a while, it was the only course in the country where golfers could play one round in two states.

www.gateway-lodge.com
715-547-3321
•

MICHIGAN

Deej has a green thumb and a green cottage.

RONORA LODGE AND RETREAT CENTER
Watervliet, Michigan

We sit by candlelight on a roomy screened porch as night arrives with its choir of tree frogs and crickets. Only forest, fields and river surround us in this isolated but simple roost for the night. It is Lonnie's Eco Cottage, an octagon-shaped cedar cabin with artistic touches, including pottery made by proprietors Deej and Hunter Leggitt.

The cottage is a part of the 350-acre Ronora Lodge and Retreat Center, a former camp for girls that was long past its prime when the Leggitts took over. Other lodging options are more straightforward: simple dorm rooms, cottages with kitchens, a lodge with ten bedrooms, sundeck and handsome fieldstone fireplace.

At the eco cottage, we drink from a water cooler, since only unfiltered rainwater comes out of kitchen and bathroom taps. We sleep long and deep on a firm mattress, windows open and ceiling fan gently humming.

We use a composting toilet. An on-demand water heater produces steamy showers in a snap. A one-burner stove runs on alcohol. Sunlight pours through the many windows, minimizing the need for artificial light.

Visitors can schedule equine therapy activities for people, or groups can just rent facilities and come up with their own itinerary. On the grounds are hiking trails and a private lake.

Deej (of Shawnee descent) and Hunter (a Unitarian minister) follow a raw food diet. Groups that arrange a stay that includes meals don't have to go this route, but it's an option. An organic vegetable garden and foraged foods are the foundation of the owners' diet.

Our raw food dinner was a fine and filling meal of pumpkin seed pesto with spaghetti squash, other raw vegetables, walnut pesto crackers and dips made from sun-dried tomatoes and purslane. The meal ended with blended grapefruit juice, blueberries and hot peppers in one drink.

The guest chef was Adam Graham of Florida, here to speak at a Ronora raw food conference. He was smitten with the retreat after helping to scout out sites for the movie *Love and Action in Chicago*, part of which was filmed here.

Ronora Lodge and Retreat Center
9325 Dwight Boyer Road
Watervliet, Michigan
www.ronoralodge.com 269-463-6315
•

The porch view from Lonnie's Eco Cottage

The MiSo house of tomorrow produces more energy than it uses, today.

MORE GREEN PLACES TO VISIT

The shiny aluminum **MiSo** (Michigan Solar) house—designed by University of Michigan students for a nationwide Solar Decathlon in 2005—is open occasionally for tours at **Matthaei Botanical Gardens**, 1800 N. Dixboro Road, Ann Arbor. The 650-square-foot structure generates more electricity (from solar panels) than it uses and was designed as a prototype for compact, affordable and sustainable housing. Skylights stretch nearly to the floor in arches that lessen the need for artificial light. Simply furnished, with a sleek Euro and Space Age feel, it resembles an Airstream trailer without wheels.

www.mbgna.umich.edu 734-647-7600

•

At **Boyne Resorts**, 1 Boyne Mountain Road, Boyne Falls, proprietary snow making equipment maximizes snow output with less compressed air. So snow guns are about 40 percent more efficient that previous models, and the result is lighter, fluffier artificial snow that requires a lower level of natural resources. The addition of 90 Boyne Low-E snow guns in 2010 meant that more ski areas were open for business earlier than usual.

www.boyneresorts.com 231-549-6000

•

"Our girls even have their own nutritionist," the William Calder family declares, referring to the 138 milk cows at **Calder Dairy and Farms**, 9334 Finzel Road, Carleton. Milk bottling and deliveries began in 1946, but now the three-generation family farm supplies most of the milk, instead of relying on surrounding dairy farms. Visitors are welcome, and the farm store sells goodies, from ice cream to pickles.

www.calderdairy.com 734-654-2622

•

The **Ford Rouge Factory Tour**, which begins at 20900 Oakwood Boulevard, Dearborn, shows off what the car manufacturer says is the world's largest living roof, a 10.4-acre garden on top of the final assembly area for Ford F-150 trucks. A view from an 80-foot-tall deck is one of five tour components. In addition, an outdoor "living laboratory" walking tour, which explains the area's environmental transformation, is offered from April to October. A sophisticated rainwater treatment system, skylights, light monitors and other eco-aggressive features earn the Rouge a LEED gold rating.

www.thehenryford.org 800-835-5237

•

Tart cherries draw a crowd in Leelanau County, Michigan, which grows more of them than anyplace else on the planet. That means a visit to **Cherry Republic**, 6026 S. Lake Street, Glen Arbor, is mandatory, for its cherry lemonade, burgers with cherries, chicken salad with dried cherries (served on cherry bread), a dozen kinds of cherry ice cream and scads of canned, bottled and jarred cherry products (sweets to alcohol). Owner Bob Sutherland says he'll never nationally franchise the Glen Arbor retail/cafe/bakery operation. "This store belongs here—not in Washington or Rhode Island."

That said, he's opened two smaller stores in Michigan: Cherry Republic Embassy, 150 E. Front Street, Traverse City; and Cherry Republic Outpost, 411 Bridge Street, Charlevoix.

www.cherryrepublic.com 800-206-6949

•

Contemplate the sculpture at the Frederik Meijer Gardens and Sculpture Park.

Within 132 acres of meadows to woodlands are more than 30 imposing sculptures on 30 acres of the **Frederik Meijer Gardens and Sculpture Park**, 1000 E. Beltline NE, Grand Rapids. The sculptures are the work of globally known artists who represent an array of styles and historical eras, including Auguste Rodin, Henry Moore and Deborah Butterfield.

www.meijergardens.org 888-957-1580

•

The Snooty Fox, 13416 Red Arrow Highway, Harbert, wants to satisfy your craving for the outdoors without making you sleep on the ground. So it offers "glamping"—glamorous camping, which consists of a simple cabin with electricity, bunk beds (the bottom one can sleep two) and a clean bathroom that you walk to but don't have to share. Sheets and towels are included. Gather around the fire pit after sunset. There's also a lodge for cooking and group retreats.

www.snootyfox.com 269-426-5101

•

Head to the barn for a filling meal at **Pond Hill Farm**, 5581 S. Lake Shore Drive, Harbor Springs. Meats, veggies, eggs are products of the farm. So are many of the sauces and preserves, canned on-site. Nibble on crackers spread with cream cheese and pepper jelly (a popular specialty), then buy more of what you've eaten at the barn's ground-level farm store. Barn dances, elegant farm-to-table dinners and u-pick berry gathering also happen here. Feed the farm fish (trout) and visit livestock (chickens to sheep), or fling a big butternut or acorn into the fields, via the Squash Rocket—a big slingshot.

www.pondhill.com 231-526-FARM

•

What's cooking at **Mia and Grace Bakery and Bistro**, 1133 Third Street, Muskegon? Just look at the strips of plain brown paper that hang on the wall. They make it easy for chef-owners Jeremy and Jamie Paquin, a husband-wife team, to replace one item with another as batches and key ingredients dwindle.

Mia and Grace's features a fresh and ever-changing menu.

Sodas and ice cream (my choices included garlic) are made on the premises. Order a hot dog, and a link almost as thick as a half-ring of bologna arrives; it's another Paquin product, dressed up with housemade ketchup, rosemary mustard and pickled onions. Dinner entrée options depend upon the day, but pecan-crusted trout with organic black rice and smoked apples is among the possibilities.

www.miaandgrace.com
231-725-9500

•

Enveloped in 60,000 acres of wilderness is **Porcupine Mountains Folk School**, which offers both one-day classes, such as soap or lotion making, and longer term instruction in building a timber frame structure. The work takes place in the former carpentry shop of Porcupine Mountains Wilderness State Park, near Ontonagon.

www.porkies.org 906-885-5545

•

Sample the pear brandy, dine or stay at Black Star Farms.

Michigan's first certified organic restaurant is **Mind, Body and Spirits,** 301 S. Main Street, Rochester, whose "inspired dining" slogan is about ecologically sound structure and locally grown food. A century-old building with geothermal heating/cooling, solar power, a greenhouse and other enhancements shows that owner Mike Flesz treads lightly on the planet. A meal here can turn into a field trip.

www.mindbodyspirits.com 248-651-3663

•

A plant-filled roof with colorful and hardy sedums tops the **Curious Kids' Discovery Zone at Silver Beach**, 333 Broad Street, St. Joseph. Natural insulation from the roof means lower heating and cooling costs for the building, which overlooks Lake Michigan. Children learn about horticulture at this city's second Curious Kids location.

www.curiouskidsmuseum.com 269-982-8500

•

Pear in a bottle. Many enterprises in Michigan produce wine, beer or spirits, but only **Black Star Farms**, 10844 E. Revold Road, Suttons Bay, sells a pear brandy whose bottle also contains a Bartlett. A winery, distillery, inn, cafe and creamery make this a one-stop destination for getting acquainted with some of the state's best agricultural products.

www.blackstarfarms.com 231-944-1251

•

Crystal Spa, a part of **Crystal Mountain Resort**, 12500 Crystal Mountain Drive, Thompsonville, was the first spa in the Midwest to earn LEED certification. The generous use of local artwork, sustainable building materials, large windows and an emphasis on local food helped the facility earn this distinction.

www.crystalmountain.com
231-378-2000

•

Top of the crop among ice cream shops. That's how Jon and Nancy Plummer's **Moomers**, 7263 N. Long Lake Road, Traverse City, ranked after a *Good Morning America* online poll of ice cream lovers. About twenty of the farmstead shop's 100-plus flavors are available daily. Your own wild ideas about creamy combos are welcome. The lengthy roundup of specialty sundaes includes the Wholey Cow: 10 scoops, "every topping we have," bananas, brownies and "an entire can of whipped cream."

www.moomers.com 231-941-4122

•

Whitefish tacos at The Cooks' House

A crunch from cabbage and kick from chipotle mayo zip up whitefish tacos at **The Cooks' House**, 115 Wellington Street, Traverse City. It was a tight squeeze for diners until it consolidated around the block with a second restaurant owned by chefs Eric Patterson and Jennifer Blakeslee. Why merge? The owners know that life is short, and that "more" doesn't always spell heightened happiness. They prefer to buy from local farmers and artisans. Whitefish caviar, braised pork belly, rutabaga-potato mash, pickled green beans and more make the menu.

www.thecookshouse.net
231-946-8700

•

Michigan ranks as the second most agriculturally diverse state (after California), thanks to the many microclimates that exist within the Wolverine State. These food celebrations hint at the array of bounty, and the enthusiasm for being national in scope.

National Asparagus Festival, Hart. Held throughout Oceana County during the second weekend of June, in an area whose sandy soil is attractive for growing the crop (although California and Washington grow more).
www.nationalasparagusfestival.org

•

National Blueberry Festival, South Haven. Held in mid August, in the World's Highbush Blueberry Capitol (Maine leads in lowbush berry production).
www.blueberryfestival.com

•

National Cherry Festival, Traverse City. A weeklong celebration in early July that began in 1926. The area leads the world in tart cherry production, growing about 75 percent of the U.S. crop. www.cherryfestival.org

•

National Morel Festival, Boyne City. Held in mid May, with outings to coach novices about how to find the often-elusive fungi. Since the morel is a wild food, national production stats don't exist.
www.morelfest.com

•

National Pickle Festival, Linwood. Held in mid August. Michigan leads the nation in pickling cucumber production.
www.linwoodpicklefestival.com

•

National Strawberry Festival, Belleville. Held in June since 1976 as a way to promote the state's crop while raising funds for local nonprofit organizations. (California, Florida, Oregon and New York are frontrunners in production nationwide.)
www.nationalstrawberryfest.com

•

National Trout Festival, Kalkaska. Held since 1933 to coincide with the spring opening of trout season. The celebration began as a holiday because the community used to simply close most businesses to go fishing.
www.nationaltroutfestival.com

Learn to bake in an outdoor oven at North House Folk School, Grand Marais, Minnesota (page 102).

MINNESOTA

N

Ely
pg 95

Grand Marais
pg 98

1

61

59

Ogema
pg 120

White Earth Lake
pg 125

Duluth
pg 92

35

94

North Branch
pg 125

Franconia
pg 125

St. Paul
pg 114

Montevideo
pg 116

94

59

212

Minneapolis
pg 108

Red Wing
pg 125

New Ulm
pg 118

35

Wabasha
pg 122

61

14

14

90

90

Lanesboro
pg 104

MINNESOTA

A St. Paul cafe rewards its neighborhood. Nature centers protect eagles, bears and wolves. A folk art school teaches bygone heritage and craftsmanship.

SOLGLIMT LAKESHORE B&B

Duluth, Minnesota

Many people who vacation in Duluth find their way to the Duluth Lakewalk, which extends 4.2 miles, along shoreline and through parks. Duluth's iconic Aerial Lift Bridge looms near the Lakewalk's southern end, at the St. Louis River. Crowds know when to gather to watch the monstrous bridge deck rise, thanks to the *Duluth Shipping News*, which lists arrival and departure times for ships, plus home port and cargo. The operation might occur more than 40 times a day during summer.

Two blocks on the other side of the bridge is Solglimt (Danish for "glistening sun") Lakeshore B&B. Here you'll find a peaceful and ecologically progressive all-suite bed-and-breakfast on the sandy isle of Park Point. When Brian and Mary Grover started their B & B, it was a humble two-room cabin. Now it's a sleek and homey, five-suite inn.

Park Point has a seven-mile beach to roam, some of which passes through a conservancy and century-old pine forest, part of St. Louis River

Solglimt's inviting living/dining room has a whimsical touch:
a painted line and scissors to show the new doorway.

MINNESOTA

Estuary. Park Point and adjacent Wisconsin Point (three miles long) form the world's longest freshwater sandbar.

Room rates include a three-course breakfast of fresh food. A recent summertime menu listed lemon-apricot scones with lemon curd; a chilled soup of diced strawberries, vanilla yogurt, orange juice and honey; green eggs (a blanched spinach scramble) atop slices of organic ham (with Brian expertly shaping ribbons of tomato into rose-like garnishes).

In the spirit of this green neighborhood, the patio path is sandstone and cobblestone, recycled from a road construction project. Much of the inn's décor—woodwork, hand railings, exterior stone—is salvaged material from a Park Point school. Other components emphasize sustainability (bamboo floors, dual-flush toilets) without relinquishing the luxury of jetted bathtubs, waterfront picture windows and in-room fireplaces. Worms—vermicomposting—turn table scraps into compost to enrich the soil in the inn's organic, award-winning garden.

A bike path runs past the front of their house, and the backyard makes prime seating for Lake Superior's theatrics. "The lake usually gives a good show," Mary says, of ships approaching the Aerial Lift Bridge or the drama of stormy weather. "Staying here is not cheap, but we try to give our guests the best value possible."

Solglimt Lakeshore B&B
828 Lake Avenue South
Duluth, Minnesota
www.solglimt.com 877-727-0596
•

Take a stroll along Park Point's seven-mile beach.

More green places to visit in Duluth:

See how the Amazon River's ecosystem differs from ours in the Midwest at the **Great Lakes Aquarium**, 353 Harbor Drive, devoted to the display and stewardship of freshwater habitats.

www.glaquarium.org 218-740-FISH

•

Order smoked Cajun salmon by the pound or by the sandwich at **Northern Waters Smokehaus**, 394 Lake Avenue South, which has been featured on the Food Network's "Diners, Drive-ins and Dives" series. Great Lakes fish, bacon, bison and other meats are smoked in small batches. Proprietor Eric Goerdt honed his skills as a fisherman while living in Alaska. All his meats, fish and poultry come from local sources.

www.nwsmokehaus.com
888-663-7800

Northern Waters sells fresh smoked meats, and fish caught in Lake Superior.

INTERNATIONAL WOLF CENTER

Ely, Minnesota

Wolves can hear a howl ten miles away. That tidbit comes out during "Wolf 101," a regular presentation about the species at the International Wolf Center, on the outskirts of Ely. I learn that a wolf can eat 20 percent of its body weight in one sitting, and that it would be unusual to see a red wolf outside of North Carolina. The Great Plains gray wolf inhabits the Midwest, but not all of them are gray.

Taxidermy mounts show wolves in life-like stances: playing, hunting, defending themselves. The Little Wolf exhibit follows a pup during its first year of life. The Wolves and Humans area explains how much we've misunderstood them.

Four wolves—Grizzer, Maya, Denali and Aidan—roam their enclosed 1.25-acre home and sometimes are visible through the observation windows in the auditorium. Other, elderly wolves live in retirement quarters, which means they are protected from the younger animals and are not as visible (although a Web cam and remote video system show both wolf environments).

This nonprofit attraction exists to advance "the survival of wolf populations by teaching about wolves, their relationship to wild lands and the human role in their future."

For a more intimate experience, staffers arrange occasional auditorium slumber parties for participants. Wolf tracking and wolf den work weekends also are scheduled, as are seminars for educators and college students.

International Wolf Center
1369 Highway 169
Ely, Minnesota
www.wolf.org 218-365-4695

•

*Gray wolves are well suited
to the cold Minnesota winters.*

Don't worry—you get to be on the other side of the glass.

NORTH AMERICAN BEAR CENTER

Ely, Minnesota

Wolf Creek Pass, Clear Lake, Wilderness Wind: This is the signage en route to Ely.

Three fat ravens feast on road kill. Logging operations are ongoing inside Superior National Forest.

It seems fitting that the North American Bear Center makes its home in such a resource-rich environment. Although the big focus is on black bears, all eight living species of bear receive attention.

Visitors watch a trio of black bears—Ted, Honey and Lucky—through a large wall of glass or from an upstairs observation deck. They live in two acres of enclosed forest (with pond and waterfalls), which means they are able to forage to supplement food delivered by staff.

Amazingly, people had tried to raise these bears as pets. The youngest, Lucky, was on the verge of being killed because his owners decided he was unmanageable.

Indoor exhibits, taxidermy, videos and presentations aim to separate bear facts from fiction. Example: About 70 percent of human deaths from grizzly bears are by mothers defending cubs, but black bear mothers have not been known to kill anyone in defense of cubs.

Some features, like the Cub Room, are specifically designed for children, who can watch videos of wild bears: One removes a heavy rock while digging a den. Another plays with her cub.

"We have a small miracle team that runs everything here," says Donna Andrews, manager and curator. Staff and volunteers are inspired, in part, by feedback from Facebook and an online "den cam," where animal lovers follow the daily rhythms of bears living in the wild. Lynn Rogers, a bear biologist, posts updates.

"Schools all over the world watch us, have done projects about bears and sent us murals and thank you cards," Donna says.

In general, bears have been "unfairly demonized for centuries," the nonprofit enterprise asserts. The animal's moaning is an expression of fear but might be misinterpreted as anger. Its purr is a sign of satisfaction.

Donna compares the study of bears to people: "Even three captive bears can teach us about behavior, their needs, their preferences." Like us, they often elevate their heads while napping or put their food on a log—their table—before eating.

Admission to the bear center is free, but donations are appreciated. No grants or government funds subsidize operations.

North American Bear Center
1926 Highway 169
Ely, Minnesota
www.bear.org 877-365-7879
•

The cafe has the perfect setting for enjoying a drink and a meal in Grand Marais.

ANGRY TROUT CAFE

Grand Marais, Minnesota

"Show your trout" to get a free dinner for two, the challenge begins, but there is a catch and it has nothing to do with fishing.

I am at the Angry Trout Cafe, a converted commercial fishing shanty in the harbor of Grand Marais. The place definitely has an attitude but little fury that I can see.

There is plenty of time to get acquainted, while waiting for a table as sunset beckons. So I learn about the free dinners, given after magnetic signs that say "trout" are displayed on a vehicle's doors for 60 days, but don't even think about participating unless your mode of transportation gets at least 40 miles per gallon. That's a requirement for this incentive.

Owners George Wilkes and Barb LaVigne are not interested in having just anybody advertising their business. They also are blunt and fervent about their priorities and business philosophy in other ways.

"Although the function of the Angry Trout is to serve our customers, our purpose, which is a broader concern, is to make money in a way that makes a better world for ourselves, other people, other life on earth and for future generations," states the menu.

"To do this, we will attempt to consider all of our costs of operation, including the environmental and social costs now and in the future that have traditionally been omitted from the evaluation of economic success."

What does this mean? Plenty, and the menu provides great detail. Beer comes from kegs, "to avoid the waste of all those bottles." Shrimp are spot prawns, caught through trapping, not trawling, in Alaskan waters. Most vegetables and meats are organic; farms are listed by name and location.

Trout chowder and tomato fennel soup are specials when I visit, and the fresh fish choices are Lake Superior herring, lake trout and whitefish, caught and processed by the adjacent Dockside Fish Market.

Appetizer choices include herring caviar (served with crackers, herbed sour cream and fruit), smoked fish (served with regional cheeses and horseradish cranberry sauce) and deep-fried fish fritters.

The vibe is casual, the service attentive, the prices affordable, but not cheap. I read about who hand-harvests the wild rice and who hand-carved the entry door. I also learn which area residents made the salt and pepper shakers, the credit card trays, the organic cotton napkins, light fixtures, bathroom mosaics and stained glass. Outdoor chairs used to be tractor seats. Indoor furnishings are made from 15 types of local trees. Scrappy cardboard menu covers are pieces of boxes that held food or beverages.

Unless I protest—and why would I?—74 percent of my tip goes to the server and the rest is divided among kitchen staff. Carry-out food orders arrive on a reusable tray that should be returned, or the customer can bring her own container.

The absence of Coke or Pepsi products is intentional. The restaurant's electricity comes from wind power, and the neighborhood emotionally fuels the place in myriad other ways.

Want to learn more about this rabidly sustainable business, which is open May to mid-October? Order the *Angry Trout Cafe Notebook: Friends, Recipes and the Culture of Sustainability*, written by George in 2004.

Angry Trout Cafe
408 Highway 61
Grand Marais, Minnesota
www.angrytroutcafe.com 218-387-1265
•

NANIBOUJOU LODGE
Grand Marais, Minnesota

The ground-level interior of Naniboujou Lodge is painted in the deeply rich colors and patterns of the Cree Indians. This includes every inch of the 20-foot domed ceiling in the dining room, the work of French artist Antoine Goufce in art deco style. The dining room also contains the largest fireplace made of native stone in Minnesota; it's 20 feet high and weighs 200 tons.

The lodge pops up out of nowhere along the Lake Superior shoreline and was named after the Cree god of the outdoors. It opened in 1929 as an exclusive getaway, whose charter members included Babe Ruth and Jack Dempsey, but the Great Depression compromised the project's success. Despite numerous changes in ownership, Naniboujou remains an affordable destination in a beautiful location.

If you can't spend the night, make reservations for a meal, or drop in for high tea in the afternoon. Breakfast options include wild rice whole wheat toast, wild rice sausage, and wild rice instead of potatoes with omelets.

Naniboujou Lodge
20 Naniboujou Trail
Grand Marais, Minnesota
www.naniboujou.com 218-387-2688

•

MINNESOTA

(left) The dining room is an imaginative meld of art deco and Cree Indian art.

North House Folk School's warehouses were constructed in the 1930s by the CCC.

NORTH HOUSE FOLK SCHOOL

Grand Marais, Minnesota

Forty miles south of the Canadian border, a Minnesota village of 1,400 overlooks a shore of near-paradise.

"We're a long way from everywhere," observes Greg Wright, and most people who stay for more than a vacation "don't come here by accident."

It is the same with many of the students at his North House Folk School, where traditional northern crafts and ways of life are taught. Students leave with more than wall hangings and harbor photography.

Imagine thinking like an Inuit when building your own kayak or sculpting art from sandstone. Weave strips of bark into baskets, shoes, hats—or make a birch bark canoe. Make mukluks from moose hide and canvas, or drums from cedar and rawhide.

Learn blacksmithing, bladesmithing and flintknapping. Make sausage, a wood stove, yurt or earthen oven. Become a student of solar power or herbal health care. Wood turning—using a lathe to shape wood into a bowl—is a Scandinavian-inspired process taught here. A fall class focuses on wild rice, from harvesting to hulling.

Many of the classes "celebrate cultural traditions, the things that bind us together over time," says Greg, the nonprofit school's executive director. Teachers "find joy in creating with their hands and connecting with the northern landscape."

The school emerged from "a community already rich in the arts." About 13,000 people from 36 states and three foreign countries found their way to North House in 2009.

Most instruction occurs in warehouses built by the Civilian Conservation Corps in the 1930s. When the buildings became eyesores, they were given to the community. Then came proposals to level the property and build condos, open a museum or transform the structures into artists' studios.

The folk school idea was floated and received a six-month trial run. "They hoped for 100 students and got 200," Greg explains. Now the campus also includes converted fishing buildings and harbor docks.

The folk school philosophy emphasizes learning and creating, not grades or competition. Tuition reductions are possible, in exchange for labor. Students arrange their own meals and lodging. Choices include campsites, cottages, motels, bed-and-breakfast inns.

Craft and wood-fired baking demos, Norwegian fjord horse-and-cart lessons and sailing lessons on a 50-foot traditionally rigged schooner occur at least weekly during summer and early autumn.

North House Folk School
500 Highway 61 West
Grand Marais, Minnesota
www.northhouse.org
888-387-9762
•

A teacher's amusing critters are used to inspire a wool felting class.

Adrienne Sweeney stands in the theater with hand-me-down seats from the Guthrie.

COMMONWEAL THEATRE COMPANY
Lanesboro, Minnesota

At Commonweal Theatre donors get their name on a Mason jar and fill it with whatever they choose. The Donor Pantry wall has rows of jars that hold photos, paintbrushes, golf tees, messages and other mementos. It's typical of the novel thinking that seems to come naturally in Lanesboro, population 800.

Lanesboro is known as the Bed and Breakfast Capital of Minnesota.

More than one dozen B&Bs do business in this part of far southeast Minnesota, and many are historic downtown Victorians. Others overlook swoops of farmland, river or forested bluffs. Bicyclists on the 60-mile, paved Root River Trail (www.rootrivertrail.org) account for some of the tourist business. Others come to canoe, fish or hike along the limestone bluffs, which reach up to 300 feet high.

A consignment shop—the nonprofit Lanesboro Local Marketplace, in a refurbished gas station—is devoted to food, art, fishing lures, goat milk soap and other products made locally.

"It's something we talked about for 20 years," says Linda Hazel, store manager, but the business didn't open until the local grocery store closed and an $8,000 grant reduced startup costs. Now about 60 vendors within 50 miles of Lanesboro participate.

Commonweal Theatre Company began with summer-only performances. Now the regional theater operates April to December, with a season that mixes classics, performance premieres and (always) a Henrik Ibsen play. The venue—a former cheese factory furnished and decorated with a conglomeration of recycled materials—is not your typical playhouse.

Pyrex plates and cookware lids are embedded into doors. Rusty heads of hammers turn into door handles. Barn doors are bathroom stalls. Cattle stanchions are coatracks.

The 186 theater seats are pleasantly garish hand-me-downs from the Guthrie Theater in Minneapolis. Suspended from the lobby ceiling are a bed frame and eclectic mix of other items: banged-up shovels, plungers, pitchforks and other everyday implements.

"These are the props of normal people's lives, and historical to the region," says Adrienne Sweeney, the theater's marketing director. Much of the scrapyard artistry is the work of Karl Unnasch, a local sculptor who specializes in the use of reclaimed and salvaged materials.

Lanesboro used to have its own thriving opera, flour mills and horse races, but things changed when the Milwaukee Railroad rerouted its tracks, leaving the community to die. When it was nicknamed "Sewer City" the residents fought back.

They persuaded the National Register of Historic Places to list the downtown. In 1998, Lanesboro won a Great American Main Street Award from the National Trust for Historic Preservation.

In more recent years, Lanesboro ranked among the nation's 50 best outdoor sports towns (*Sports Afield* magazine) and 20 best "dream towns" in which to live and play (*Outside* magazine).

Commonweal Theatre Company
208 Parkway Avenue North
Lanesboro, Minnesota
www.commonwealtheatre.org 800-657-7025
•

EAGLE BLUFF ENVIRONMENTAL LEARNING CENTER

Lanesboro, Minnesota

The two tenants are unlikely partners, but they have something in common: a need to connect with nature.

In one building are participants in Stringwood, a two-week summer chamber music program for ages 12 to 18. "This is a sanctuary, a place to offer deep learning," says co-founder Ray Shows. "Our mission is to educate the next generation of chamber musicians."

Elsewhere, Scheels, a Midwest sporting goods retailer, presents archery and black powder firearms instruction. "It's the perfect place to train people to be an outdoor expert in many of our specialty areas—archery, hunting, camping," says Garth Caselli of Scheels University.

There is room for both groups and more at Eagle Bluff Environmental Learning Center, three miles north of Lanesboro. Minnesota has six nonprofit, accredited environmental learning centers. Eagle Bluff is the newest and the only one that is not in the northern part of the state.

"There was a void in this area," says Joe Deden, Eagle Bluff's executive director and a trained forester. "Kids were being driven seven hours north for this type of experience."

Field trips and workshops connect children to nature at Eagle Bluff's 80 acres, surrounded by thousands of acres of state forest. For some students, especially those from poor and urban areas, this is a life-changing experience.

Adults come to Eagle Bluff on group retreats, take classes or use the ropes course as a team-building exercise. Chefs prepare and serve gourmet meals after talks about living off the grid, the effects of pesticides like Atrazine or some other environmental topic.

"There are few places that are about the wild anymore," notes Joe's wife, Mary Bell. "You hear the sounds of society, you see the lights. Here, we are surrounded by bluffs and diversity of species. It still has an element of 'quiet' and 'wild.'"

Joe and colleague Jeff Kamm also lead Old Buzzard Birding Ecotours in May and June.

Eagle Bluff Environmental Learning Center
28097 Goodview Drive
Lanesboro, Minnesota
www.eagle-bluff.org 507-467-2437
•

Also in the neighborhood, 10 miles southwest of Lanesboro:

Fly fisherman find sound advice about building rods and tying flies at the **National Trout Learning Center**, 120 Anthony Street, Preston. Why here? Limestone bedrock maintains water temperature at 46 to 48 degrees and holds oxygen well, making it the perfect environment for all three species of trout—rainbow, brown and brook.

Preston may be the epicenter of trout fishing because of a highly unusual geological karst, which is a landscape of limestone caves, streams and fissures. The area has hundreds of springfed creeks, rich with minerals and cooled by limestone.

Local fishing guides and others address questions about where fish are biting. Many streams are accessible to the public, even though they are on private land.

Why go "national" in the facility title? "We think we can hold our own and felt we should capture the label and live up to it," says George Spangler, a retired fisheries biologist and University of Minnesota professor who moved to Preston because of his love of fishing.

www.nationaltroutlearningcenter.org 507-765-4700
•

Take the Flour Tower elevator to the top floor for a great view of Minneapolis.

MILL CITY MUSEUM

Minneapolis, Minnesota

One of the Twin Cities' most dynamic museums is about flour power, resilience, reputation and ruins.

The Mill City Museum, on the banks of the Mississippi River, is a candid, airy and fascinating testimonial to what used to be the world's largest flour mill and the city that produced the most flour.

The story of the Washburn A Mill, which became General Mills in 1928, is told by average mill workers. Visitors hear their recorded voices as they ride an eight-story freight elevator, which stops periodically to show various stages of flour production.

We learn that, until 1930, Minneapolis produced more flour than any city in the world. Washburn A opened in 1880 and closed abruptly in 1965, with many workers hearing the news from television instead of their boss.

We listen to women who worked the line during wartime, until "the men came home from service to take the jobs away from us," and how heavy flour bags were transported by hand into railroad cars—175 railcars of wheat processed per day. We hear how sweat and flour dust formed a "goop" that had to be scraped from the arms of mill workers. Some made $25 per week and considered themselves lucky.

Explosions devastated Washburn A twice while it was a working mill. The third time the building went up in flames, in 1991, it was housing the homeless.

The museum was built in and around the mill ruins, which stand as a memorial to the turbulent but proud past. In their heyday, 26 flour mills operated on the Minneapolis riverfront. The last, Pillsbury A Mill, closed in 2003.

What made Minneapolis such a hub for flour production, and why isn't it that way anymore? That's part of the story, too, as are the food products that became known worldwide because of General Mills and Pillsbury.

A replica test kitchen is part of this museum, and it smells great because brownies and breads are baked (and sampled) throughout the day.

The Flour Tower freight elevator ride ends at a rooftop observation deck that offers tremendous views of the river. Nearby is St. Anthony Falls and urban riverfront development.

At ground level, you can hear early radio spots and watch TV ads for Malt-O-Meal, Wheaties and Bisquick. You can see how Betty Crocker's looks get updated with the times.

Vintage product packaging, equipment, ads and attitudes are grouped for comparison. In the Water Lab, kids can wear waterproof aprons or get wet while learning how the river has been used to move logs and other commodities.

This museum has exhibits to entertain schoolchildren, farmers, factory workers, white-collar executives and anyone who likes to cook.

Mill City Museum
704 S. Second Street
Minneapolis, Minnesota
www.millcitymuseum.org 612-341-7555

•

MINNESOTA

Red Stag Supper Club
Minneapolis, Minnesota

News, to me: Energy and water account for 30 to 40 percent of the average restaurant's operating budget. Reduce these expenses, and it's good business as well as good for the planet.

Red Stag Supper Club, the first LEED-certified restaurant in Minnesota, cuts energy bills in half and saves 70 percent on its water bill because of an eco-savvy design in a former industrial warehouse in its northeast Minneapolis neighborhood. Seating cushions are stuffed with ribbons of tape from many, many discarded cassettes. Dining tables are doors recycled from a condo project. The marble bar comes from a hotel. Corn is a key ingredient in the carpeting.

MINNESOTA

Red Stag was the first LEED-certified restaurant in Minneapolis.

"Supper club," in this location, is more about "bringing people together for interaction and community" than big-as-your-plate steaks served after an hour's wait for a table, says Lauren Schuppe, Red Stag manager (but she adds that owner Kim Bartmann, a Wisconsin native, has fond memories of traditional, rural supper club fare).

At the Red Stag, chefs will make their own sausage, pickle 50 pounds of ramps and boil down bushels of homegrown heirloom tomatoes so that a rich and locally sourced pasta sauce is available in the dead of winter. A majority of the menu's ingredients come from within 60 miles of the restaurant.

Corned beef hash arrives with parsnips and carrots. An herbal hollandaise sauce transforms poached eggs into a clever Green Eggs and (smoked) Ham. Sometimes ingredients deviate from what's local, and results are extraordinary: Consider the chunks of lobster and avocado in the house egg salad sandwich.

Cheap Date night, on Tuesdays, means a couple can order two entrées, dessert and a bottle of wine for $32. A block party in August draws together the music of local bands, roller skaters and hula hoop contestants.

Red Stag Supper Club
509 First Avenue NE
Minneapolis, Minnesota
www.redstagsupperclub.com
612-767-7766
•

Green arts in the neighborhood:

The neighborhood enjoys a flourishing arts district whose anchor is **Casket Arts**, a coalition of 100 artists and art-related businesses. Open studio and gallery tours occur monthly, from 5 to 9 p.m. on the first Thursday. Much of the studio space fills a former casket factory, at 681 Seventeenth Avenue NE.
More at www.casketarts.com.

The Minnesota Twins' new home scores a LEED silver certificate.

TARGET FIELD

Minneapolis, Minnesota

Fans of Target Field, home to the Minnesota Twins, seem to talk up four things more than anything else:

Fresh air. The new baseball stadium's open-air design replaces the stuffy Metrodome, the enclosed, musty and annoying echo chamber where the Twins played for 28 years.

The view. The city skyline looks most impressive when sitting on the third-base side. The high-definition scoreboard—57 feet high and 101 feet wide—is among the largest in professional baseball.

The layout. "Not a bad seat in the house," one fan after another declares. The closest of the 39,500 seats sits 48 feet from home plate. And there's standing room for about 1,500.

The food. Options include local products and recipes. There's walleye on a stick, wild rice soup and Red River Chili (with cubed sirloin). For vegetarians, choices include meatless burritos, kabobs and tacos.

It's easier to get to Target Field because the light rail system stops there; no other Major League Baseball park building contains a transit station. There are 827 bike parking spaces within 200 yards of Cedar Lake Trail.

OK, now we're getting warmer. What makes this facility truly unusual is the infrastructure that saves energy and lessens waste. It is the nation's second professional baseball stadium (after Nationals Park in the District of Columbia) to earn LEED certification from the U.S. Green Building Council.

Energy from a nearby garbage-burning plant fuels the stadium and its radiant heating system. Storm water is routed into a cistern, then filtered and used to irrigate the field and clean stadium seats.

A majority of the stadium's exterior was built with limestone from Mankato, just 90 miles away. Add more recycling, less energy usage, an emphasis on local products and minimized pollution and erosion. All together, they earn Target Field a LEED silver rating.

One-hour tours of the stadium happen on nongame days, Monday through Saturday. Reservations required.

Target Field
1 Twins Way
Minneapolis, Minnesota
www.minnesota.twins.com
800-33-TWINS
•

Inventive ballpark fare favors local products, like Kramarczuk sausages, at Target Field.

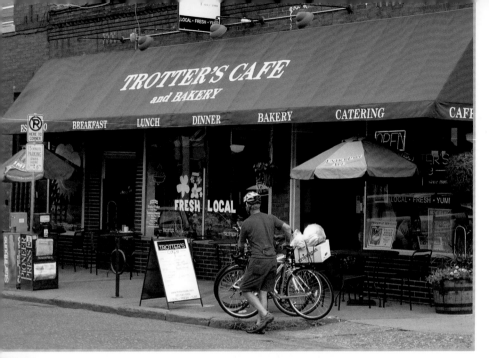

Locals in the Twin Cities have a champion at Trotter's.

MINNESOTA

TROTTER'S CAFE AND BAKERY
St. Paul, Minnesota

To Dick and Pat Trotter, sustainability means finding ways to support their Merriam Park neighborhood, halfway between the downtowns of Minneapolis and St. Paul.

They live only five blocks from work and have operated a highly regarded cafe-bakery since 1989. In addition to feeding their neighbors, they connect the community.

Saturday night is Locals Night, which means people who live within two miles of the cafe get 10 percent off their bill. Ride a bus, bike or walk to get an additional 5 percent off.

The monthly Near and Nearby Reading Series concentrates on the new works of local writers. Message boards list the local musicians who are performing, in addition to the farms whose foods are used in cooking.

"It was tough to get local products at the beginning," Dick says. "Now I have four or five farmers who come to us every week, with eggs, chicken, vegetables." "Local" used to mean within a five-state area. Now it's pretty much Minnesota and Wisconsin, with a little bit of Iowa. "I've been to many of these farms," Dick says. "I've seen the chickens, and they're not crowded into big barns. They come to me fresh—butchered on a Wednesday, here by Thursday."

Maybe that's why the chicken-pecan salad is especially popular. Other favorites are veggie burgers and buffalo burgers. One of the two daily soups is vegetarian (and often vegan). Local maple syrup and honey sweeten the muffins. Even the white and wheat flours used in baking come from Minnesota farmers.

Bring your own coffee cup or container and you'll get a discount. Cafe employees routinely donate a portion of their "counter culture" tips to non-profit causes—$2,305 over six months, when I last checked—and details are posted online.

Trotter's Cafe and Bakery
232 Cleveland Avenue North
St. Paul, Minnesota
www.trotterscafe.com 651-645-8950
•

Trotter's supports local farmers and serves as the neighborhood gathering place for social and cultural events.

Moonstone's owners forage for and grow their food.

MOONSTONE FARM

Montevideo, Minnesota

As we walk, Audrey Arner collects milkweed flowers. She will dip them into a tempura batter and deep-fry them, then add a little soy sauce or maple syrup.

Later, Audrey and her husband, Richard Handeen, marvel at the size of a hen of the woods mushroom growing in their front yard. It will be sautéed in butter, along with wild garlic scapes (the stalks of wild garlic).

"We augment a lot of our diet with wild food and teach others," Audrey says. "We don't base our cooking on what's in a recipe but on what's available."

Their 240-acre Moonstone Farm on the bluffs of western Minnesota is part prairie, part forest, with gardens of flowers

Hen of the woods grow in the front yard.

and vegetables and a pond that connects to a tributary of the Minnesota River. Beef cattle graze in pastures.

You can rent the Broodio, a one-bedroom cottage (formerly a brooder house for poultry) that incorporates solar technology. The cozy and cheerful quarters overlook the gardens and vineyard and is just a short walk from the pond, its beach and a canoe. A stay includes a continental breakfast of seasonal foods. Bathing facilities are in the main farmhouse; another option is the "charming outdoor privy, down the garden path."

Sometimes meat-eating guests buy steaks at the Carriage House, the farm store, and then cook dinner on an outdoor grill. The small shop also sells Richard's pottery, handmade brooms, farm-harvested honey and the products of others, such as cheeses, butter, wild rice and flours.

Richard is the fourth generation of his family to live here. His ancestors were Swedish immigrants who made this their home in 1872. He says, "We are slowly and continually learning what is required to live well in this place, while leaving it in even better condition than when we arrived."

Moonstone Farm
9060 Fortieth Street SW
Montevideo, Minnesota
www.moonstonefarm.net 320-269-8971

•

PUTTING GREEN ENVIRONMENTAL ADVENTURE PARK

New Ulm, Minnesota

On the day after tornado-level winds and blinding rain brought me to south central Minnesota, I was reading about "Field of Drains" and "Wetland Washing Machines" at the miniature golf course of the Putting Green, which uses signage at each hole to educate its customers about ecology and conservation.

Among the lessons:

"Rain and snowmelt soak into the ground and seep down into geological formations called aquifers."

"If all the world's water were compacted into a one-gallon jug, the fresh water would equal one tablespoon."

Field of Drains

Melting snow and heavy rains can leave pools of water in farm fields. Many fields contain networks of drains (field intakes), ditches, and underground pipes (drainage tiles) that carry water away. These networks increase the amount of productive cropland and allow farmers earlier access to their fields in the spring.

Drains and underground pipes usually empty into ditches and streams, unnaturally increasing the amount and timing of snowmelt and rainwater flow—and the eroded soil and nutrients they carry—directly into waterways. For instance, in 2001 the Blue Earth River dumped 4,510 tons of soil into the Minnesota River daily. Drainage networks can be diverted to shallow ponds created especially to slow the flow of runoff into rivers and lakes.

"One gallon of oil, if disposed of improperly, can contaminate one million gallons of water."

"With too little water, crops dry up. With too much water, crops can drown. Putt for the fields to discover the challenges involved in keeping crops growing and farms healthy."

Golfers also learn how to make ethanol from corn, how lifestyles change when water is scarce, how untreated sewage poses somber consequences—and a lot about environmental stewardship.

It's a fun and painless way to learn about conservation.

High school students did the research and writing for this nine-hole course, on nine acres in the Minnesota River Valley. Also on the grounds are a 30-foot geodesic dome for events, a solar-powered concession building, hiking trails and a two-acre garden that provides CSA shares and food for local businesses.

The project was the idea of physician Laurel Gamm, who thought the design and development of a miniature golf course would be a great way for students to learn business, art, math and physics concepts. What you see and learn are the results of teenagers' ideas and interests. High school students staff the park, which is open May to October, and also are "EcoPreneurs" who make business operation decisions.

Teens set the tone at the Putting Green.

Plans call for development of a regional and year-round sustainability education center for youth.

Putting Green Environmental Adventure Park
Valley Street and Twentieth Street South
New Ulm, Minnesota
www.puttinggreen.org 507-354-7888
•

The staff is friendly and the food is local and fresh at the remote cafe.

MINWANJIGE CAFE

Ogema, Minnesota

Much of the harvest from Minwanjige Cafe's backyard ends up in soups or salads. That includes cattail bulbs, which the locals call "swamp potatoes."

"They remind me of cucumbers," says Janice Chilton, a baker here, whose specialty is nine-grain bread. Native Americans have long known that every part of the cattail is edible or useful. Even the fluff that billows out from the plant in autumn can be used to stuff a pillow or a doll, if you're patient enough to collect it.

Big windows frame thick patches of reeds and brush at this friendly cafe, which is inside the White Earth Reservation in northwest Minnesota. For sale are products from the local roaster, Muskrat Coffee Company, along with lotions, games, pottery, wild rice products, tiny birch bark canoes and other handicrafts.

I buy a little bowl, carved from wood by cafe neighbor Harold Mentsma, and page through books written by Winona La Duke, a Native American activist who was Ralph Nader's Green Party running mate during the 1996 and 2000 elections for U.S. president.

Winona lives in the area and heads the White Earth Land Recovery Project, a nonprofit organization that works to return reservation land to the Anishinaabeg tribe, which owns about 80,000 of the reservation's 837,000 acres. The rest is under government, corporate or private ownership.

The White Earth project also strives to build strong local and sustainable food economies. This means, in part, producing and selling traditional foods: hominy, maple syrup, wild rice, jams made with local fruits. That happens under the Native Harvest label, and production happens in a former elementary school, which has a wind turbine as a backdrop. Walk-ins are welcome during business hours, when products are sold from the production area.

The area is unusual, geographically, because three diverse habitats—tall-grass prairie, hardwood and white pine—converge, luring great diversity in wildlife and vegetation. Much of this is explained at the nearby **Tamarac National Wildlife Refuge**, 35704 Highway 26, Rochert, (www.fws.gov/midwest/tamarac 218-847-2641).

"There aren't many other places in North America where this happens," says Bob Shimek, who organizes an annual Wild Food Summit (www.wildfoodsummit.org). In 2010, 100 people, from Houston to Ottawa, gathered here.

"Some people are at the investigative stage of this," Bob acknowledges, "and we accommodate all levels of interest and skill" in identifying, gathering, preparing and cooking wild foods.

His own interest in foraging "comes from having tens of thousands of acres in my backyard. That was my playground as a kid, and I learned the features and functions that this landscape has for all of us. You could go for miles with no roads or houses in sight, and I grew up with the call of the wolf just outside of my bedroom window. We are privileged to have them as neighbors here."

In this part of the Midwest, field-to-fork projects involve wild plants as well as those grown in the garden. "Reclaiming a healthy diet," Bob believes, means "reclaiming a lot of the ecological knowledge that goes with the land."

Minwanjige Cafe
33287 Highway 34
Ogema, Minnesota
www.nativeharvest.com 218-983-3834

•

Angel the eagle gets a second chance at the Eagle Center.

NATIONAL EAGLE CENTER

Wabasha, Minnesota

Angel, a bald eagle, was found on the ground, a few months after hatching. She likely survived on whatever herons dropped while feasting in nests above her. She had a broken wing that hadn't healed right, and by pure luck had escaped predators.

Surgery fixed the bone but couldn't fix her deformed muscles, so she was moved as a fledgling to Wabasha. Now she lives at the National Eagle Center, along the Mississippi River, where quick currents near the Chippewa Delta prevent river water from freezing in winter.

Hundreds of bald eagles swoop and fish in the area. Visitors can witness river life from the center's second-story observation deck and gigantic walls of windows.

Why Wabasha? Volunteers here formed Eagle Watch in 1989. Soon they became local experts who raised money to build an observation deck near the river. They also worked with like-minded groups, such as the U.S. Fish and Wildlife Service and the Sierra Club.

Visitors can watch wild eagles fly and fish on the Mississippi River.

Many communities along the Mississippi River host annual eagle watching events, but the relentless enthusiasm and emphasis on education in Wabasha eventually led to construction of the 14,000-square-foot interpretive center.

Now artwork, film clips, taped interviews and five feathered residents teach the habits, history and legends associated with the raptors.

"We have a major migratory road here," notes Bucky Flores, education program specialist. "The river's water stays open here because of our geological formation, not because of the work of a lock and dam. A strong current comes through a narrow channel, so we'll see hundreds of eagles on many winter days, especially when it's cold and just after a snowfall."

Three of the five birds that live indoors at the National Eagle Center were hit by motor vehicles as far away as California. Was'aka, whose name means "strength" in Dakota language, was found as a fledgling in Florida and is blind in one eye because of a tumor.

And then there is Angel. I met this middle-aged raptor between bath time (in the river) and mealtime (a half-pound of raw carp and sheepshead) as storm clouds rolled in. She can fly 50 to 100 feet and sometimes is placed on a longer tether, to fly outdoors between handlers.

Angel seemed content, unruffled by my gawking. Birds wear indoor tethers, and visitors get within five feet of some birds. No netting, wire mesh or glass partitions separate us, and this makes the experience more amazing than the typical wildlife rehab center.

Dakota legend has it that the largest eagles would carry the most important prayers to the heavens. Think of the words we associate with bald eagles: strength, valor, freedom.

National Eagle Center
50 Pembroke Avenue
Wabasha, Minnesota
www.nationaleaglecenter.org
877-332-4537

•

Some of the birds that live at the National Eagle Center are former residents of the **Raptor Center** at the University of Minnesota, which since 1974 has taught veterinarians raptor surgery techniques and other avian medical care. The program is home to 30 eagles, owls, falcons and hawks. Another 800 birds are treated there each year.

The university's three-year raptor medicine program is the only one like it in the world, and research enhances raptor lives in other ways. One example: Work to study and re-establish a healthy habitat for peregrine falcons led to the bird's removal from the endangered species list in 1999.

Research, rehab and public education projects also played a role in the bald eagle's removal from the endangered species list in 2007.

The Raptor Center, 1920 Fitch Avenue, St. Paul, Minnesota, is open to visitors. A tour and educational program occur on weekends.

www.raptor.cvm.umn.edu 612-624-4745.

MORE GREEN PLACES TO VISIT

Franconia Sculpture Park, 29836 St. Croix Trail, Franconia, is 20 acres of restored prairie with about 75 pieces of huge and outlandish art. Thirty to 45 artists and interns from as far away as Australia work here, turning rusty bedsprings, oil drums and other salvaged materials into bigger than life expressions of heart and humor. Admission is free.

www.franconia.org 651-257-6668

•

The **Women's Environmental Institute at Amador Hill**, 15715 River Road, North Branch, organizes retreats, lectures and other events that address environmental justice issues. On the campus is an organic demonstration garden, retreat space and other outlets for promoting sustainable living and food production.

www.w-e-i.org 651-583-0705

•

In a roomy barn that is home to **Hobgoblin Music**, 920 Highway 19, Red Wing, handcrafted folk instruments—especially Irish harps, bohrans, mountain dulcimers and banjoes—are made. Musicians perform outdoors or in the barn's upstairs loft. Workshops teach how to make your own instrument from wood, and then play music on it.

www.hobgoblin-usa.com 877-866-3936

•

Most shoreline remains undeveloped along White Earth Lake, and the early 1900s log lodge at **New Horizon Resort**, 2379 Perch Road, Waubun, offers uncluttered waterfront views. Linda May cooks up a walleye and wild rice buffet on Wednesdays, Memorial Day to Labor Day. Her husband, Chris, has taken measures to ease soil erosion and makes recycling a property-wide priority.

www.newhorizonresort.com 218-473-2138

Rock Island is a remote state park well worth a visit (page 131).

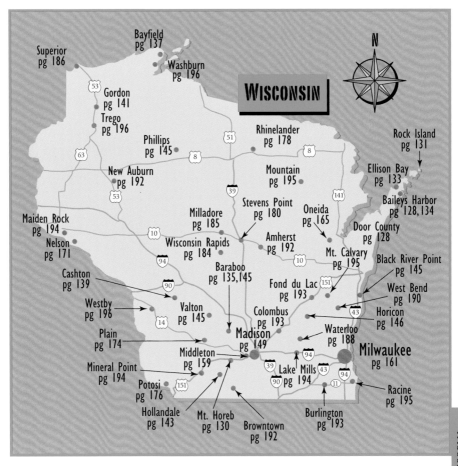

Bayfield
pg 137

Superior
pg 186

Washburn
pg 196

53 Gordon
pg 141

Trego
pg 196

WISCONSIN

N

Phillips
pg 145

51

Rhinelander
pg 178

Rock Island
pg 131

63

New Auburn
pg 192

8

8

Ellison Bay
pg 133

53

Milladore
pg 185

39

Stevens Point
pg 180

Oneida
pg 165

141

Baileys Harbor
pg 128, 134

Maiden Rock
pg 194

Nelson
pg 171

10

Wisconsin Rapids
pg 184

Amherst
pg 192

Door County
pg 128

Mt. Calvary
pg 195

Black River Point
pg 145

Cashton
pg 139

94

Baraboo
pg 135, 145

10

West Bend
pg 190

Westby
pg 196

90

Valton
pg 145

Fond du Lac
pg 193

151

43

Horicon
pg 146

Plain
pg 174

14

Colombus
pg 193

Waterloo
pg 188

Milwaukee
pg 161

Mineral Point
pg 194

Madison
pg 149

Middleton
pg 159

39

94

Potosi
pg 176

151

Lake Mills
pg 194

43

94

Hollandale
pg 143

Mt. Horeb
pg 130

90

11

Racine
pg 195

Brad

Browntown
pg 192

Burlington
pg 193

WISCONSIN

A cheesemaker figures a way to prevent whey from contaminating the Earth. Dozens of blue jeans form an American flag that hangs in a Milwaukee hotel lobby. A program that connects women with the outdoors goes international.

RIDGES SANCTUARY

Baileys Harbor, Wisconsin

Hundreds of dwarf lake irises, most no bigger than a thumbnail, grow among junipers and pop through sand at the Ridges Sanctuary in Door County. We squat in rain to examine the delicate petals, each a marvel with three splashes of deep yellow per bloom. These tiny blue-purple flowers will vanish before summer arrives.

The species is but one example of what makes these 1,400 acres at Baileys Harbor extraordinary.

"A huge number of people, even locally, don't know we exist, or think we're an exclusive country club," notes naturalist Karen Newbern. "There was a time, in the 1970s and '80s, when we didn't want visitors coming through here, and we still struggle with this now."

The Ridges is Wisconsin's oldest nonprofit nature preserve, a place of research as well as protection. Between each of 30 ridges are swales—marshy depressions—and all "create a patchwork quilt of habitats" that are unusual for a condensed area.

Dwarf lake irises are protected in Wisconsin and can be found at the Ridges Sanctuary.

Each ridge represents a former Lake Michigan shoreline, the oldest dating back 1,200 years. As shoreline recedes, vegetation sprouts and eventually morphs into boreal forests. The ridges continue to form at the water's edge, in 30- to 50-year cycles. Species tend to thrive here instead of fade away.

There's the Hine's Emerald Dragonfly, known for its brilliant green eyes and metallic body. The creature has been federally endangered since

WISCONSIN

1995, but you'll find them at the Ridges in July. Karen says no place has a bigger population than Door County.

"We're unique because such a large chunk of property has been well protected for so many years," she says. Efforts began in 1937 with the 30-acre Baileys Harbor Ridges Park, whose two range lights guide boats into the harbor.

Milwaukee botanist Albert Fuller and landscape architect Jens Jensen teamed up to prevent the area from becoming a trailer campground, a change that would have forever compromised natural habitats.

Today's big issues include neighborhood integrity and public awareness. Manure runoff from farms, beachfront lawn mowing and the threat of non-native plants—invasive species such as garlic mustard and buckthorn—are challenges. So is making more people aware of the Ridges. It heightens appreciation for nature, boosts financial support but also increases vulnerability—no matter how many boardwalks are built as footpaths.

Karen shows a simple wooden cage that protected the dwindling population of lady's slippers from deer. The device didn't prevent people from digging up this wild orchid, even though the flower rarely survives transplanting.

Five miles of hiking trails are open from dawn to dusk; a trail fee is collected. Guided field trips occur all year.

Ridges Sanctuary
8288 Highway Q
Baileys Harbor, Wisconsin
www.ridgessanctuary.org 920-839-2802

•

The Wisconsin Legislature declared 2010 as the Year of the **Niagara Escarpment**, a reference to 230 miles of often-steep ledges and cliffs that skirt through six Wisconsin counties, then underwater in Lake Michigan. The 1,000-mile escarpment—an ancient sea bottom, created through erosion before glacier movement—stretches through Ontario, Canada, and as far east as New York. The escarpment is named after the cliff over which the Niagara River plunges into Niagara Falls. For more about this geologically unique feature, see www.escarpmentnetwork.org.

•

When in Door County, look for escarpment formations along the two-mile Eagle Trail in **Peninsula State Park**. Although described as a difficult hike, it's easily managed in dry weather and when approached counterclockwise.

WISCONSIN

The Wisconsin Department of Natural Resources occasionally conducts guided hikes on Eagle Trail and dubs it the park's most spectacular trail.

www.dnr.wi.gov 920-868-3258

•

Details about the 17 other **National Natural Landmarks** in Wisconsin are at www.nature.nps.gov; the best known of the bunch is Cave of the Mounds, near Mount Horeb.

www.caveofthemounds .com 608-437-3038

The Ridges were formed by Lake Michigan's wave action over millennia. They hold microcosms of habitats and species rare elsewhere, like the Hine's Emerald Dragonfly.

Miles of beach, no motorized vehicles and great camping await.

ROCK ISLAND STATE PARK

Door County, Wisconsin

The handwritten sign says Rock Island Cafe, and the only thing on the menu is fresh berries. The sequence begins with strawberries in early July, then raspberries and thimbleberries. As summer inches into fall, blackberries ripen.

You won't see an actual restaurant, and berries are free for the taking, but you have to work for them. They grow wild in the 912 acres of Rock Island State Park. A park volunteer can show you where.

Rock Island holds the distinction of being the least-visited state park in Wisconsin, but it's not for lack of luster. It's for lack of easy access. Getting to the island requires a half-hour ferry ride from the tip of the Door County mainland to Washington Island, then a short drive, then a 15-minute ride on another ferry.

The first ferry operates all year, weather permitting, and crosses the sometimes-turbulent Death's Door passageway between Green Bay and Lake Michigan. The ferry from Washington Island to Rock Island operates Memorial Day weekend through Columbus Day.

Roughly 16,000 people visit Rock Island State Park annually. Compare that to Wisconsin's most-visited state park, Devils Lake, which gets 1.1 million visitors.

Since Rock Island is unusually remote, the park's 40 rustic campsites can be reserved. Expect outhouses, no showers, no hookups for electricity. You can buy firewood but not ice. Bring containers big enough to carry water from the well to your campsite.

Boaters who choose to moor overnight pay $1 per foot of boat length, but the water's mood swings make boating unpredictable and sometimes dangerous. Not a good match for a lightweight vessel or novice navigator.

You can explore the island on foot by hiking the six-mile perimeter, plus about four miles of crisscross trails that tend to be wide, well maintained and often shaded. Cars and bicycles are not allowed.

What is there to see? Bursts of color from wildflowers, a splendid sand beach, dolomite cliffs and see-the-bottom water are fine selling points, yet not unusual among Wisconsin parks.

One standout attraction is Potawatomi Light, the state's oldest (1836). Take off your shoes before touring this tidy little lighthouse. The view from the top will take you 20 miles away on a clear day.

An old stone water tower has been on the National Register of Historic Places since 1985. So have other quaint cobbled buildings, including the Boat House and its enormous Viking Hall, whose exhibits explain the park's history.

A wealthy Chicago man, Chester Thordarson, made his money from high voltage electrical inventions and bought Rock Island for $5,735 in 1910. He turned it into a summer estate and filled it with reminders of Icelandic and Scandinavian heritage. Elaborate hand-carved oak furniture still graces the library, and a looming fireplace will be among the widest and tallest you've ever seen.

In winter, when ice freezes between Washington and Rock, adventurous ice fishermen and cross-country skiers trek the 1.25 miles between islands. They don't get the park's blessing.

"We don't encourage people to venture onto the ice, but they do anyway," says Randy Holm, park ranger. From his perspective, Rock Island "has been discovered—we have a lot of visitors."

"You have to know what you're doing," Kirby Foss, park manager, says of the winter explorers. The park office moves to Jackson Harbor, on Washington Island, after Columbus Day, so Rock Island remains unstaffed in winter.

"Dealing with the weather, especially the northwest winds" is Kirby's biggest work challenge, but "we have a good operation" that is enhanced by Friends of Rock Island, volunteers who are passionate and active about park operations.

Tour the restored lighthouse and learn about the keepers and their families.

Midsummer is the park's busiest time, but he considers early fall another good time to visit. "We have cold, wet springs, but Lake Michigan returns its favor in September and October, when it's warmer here than in Green Bay."

Rock Island State Park
1924 Indian Road
Washington Island, Wisconsin
www.dnr.state.wi.us 920-847-2235
•

More green places to visit in Door County:

The Clearing Folk School, 12171 Garrett Bay Road, Ellison Bay, was established by landscape architect Jens Jensen in 1935 at his summer home. Jensen designed Chicago parks and the estates of well-known industrialists. The school's 130 acres of woods and meadows are within sight of Green Bay. Students connect to nature through poetry, birding, quilting,

Blacksmith Inn, viewed from the boardwalk on Baileys Harbor

philosophy and other classes. On-site accommodations discourage cell phone and computer use.

www.theclearing.org 877-854-3225

•

Genuine lovers of nature are a good fit for the 15-room **Blacksmith Inn on the Shore**, 8152 Highway 57, Baileys Harbor, where rooms overlook Lake Michigan and hammocks swing on private balconies. Follow the boardwalk over marshland, from shore to pier. Borrow a complimentary bike or kayak (snowshoes and sleds in winter). Enjoy birds and their calls while lingering in the lakefront yard.

"People who want to shop head to the other side" of the peninsula, says B&B co-owner Bryan Nelson. The more rugged east shore tends to draw a quieter and contemplative crowd.

Continental breakfast means house-made granola, fresh muffins, fresh fruit and more. Available almost anytime: popcorn and fat cherry-oatmeal cookies. Look for bakery recipes near the registration desk.

The Blacksmith Inn is adults-only lodging.

www.theblacksmithinn.com 800-769-8619

WISCONSIN

ALDO LEOPOLD LEGACY CENTER
Baraboo, Wisconsin

Preserve and protect, or expand and improve? How hard it is to do all in the name of progress.

The Aldo Leopold Shack and Farm, 264 acres that border the Wisconsin River near Baraboo, "possess exceptional value in interpreting the American experience," says Steve Adams of the National Park Service.

Aldo Leopold, professor of game management at the University of Wisconsin, bought the exhausted farm in 1935 as hunting land. Leopold and his family worked for years to plant thousands of pines and bring back the prairie. The restoration work molded the philosophy and principles for Leopold's 1949 *Sand County Almanac*, called a seminal work of the environmental movement.

It was here that Leopold realized land restoration would be his lifelong goal and legacy. It also involved family commitment. As daughter Nina Leopold Bradley explains, the Shack (a restored chicken coop) "was as close to nothing as you could get" but also "a place of great love and respect."

The area "represents a pattern of plantings and series of significant decisions that Leopold made," says Susan Flader, environmental historian. "This is a place of extraordinary integrity . . . of

Some wood used in the building comes from trees Leopold planted at his farm more than six decades ago.

Take a guided tour or even a seminar at Aldo Leopold's Shack.

visions, of processes . . . and family investment over time." Thousands of family photos and pages of writing document the transformation of this land.

Work to designate the area as a national landmark kicked in during planning for the Aldo Leopold Legacy Center, which houses administrative offices, workshop spaces and a visitor center.

Buddy Huffaker, Aldo Leopold Foundation executive director, explains, "We wanted to respect the area's character" and create "a gateway to the Shack" that would "help mitigate overuse of an exceptional site that has undergone only minimal changes since Leopold's time."

The Leopold Center teaches conservation and land ethic in a modern building that is made of pines Leopold planted. Fittingly, it was awarded the highest level—platinum—of LEED certification and was deemed greenest building in the nation.

The Leopold Center is open from May through October. See the Web site for information about guided and self-guided tours of the Shack and the Leopold Center.

Leopold Legacy Center
E13701 Levee Road
Baraboo, Wisconsin
www.aldoleopold.org 608-355-0279

•

Just seven miles west of the Leopold property is the **International Crane Foundation**, E-11376 Shady Lane Road, Baraboo, the only place in the world that offers refuge to all 15 species of cranes. The foundation also works to protect and restore habitat for cranes around the globe.

www.savingcranes.org 608-356-9462

WISCONSIN

A transformed 1885 country estate is among Wisconsin's most eco-friendly inns.

PINEHURST INN
AT PIKE'S CREEK

Bayfield, Wisconsin

Here's how Nancy Sandstrom torments herself when buying organic cotton sheets:

Where does the cotton come from? Who's picking it, and how are they treated? How far are the raw materials, and the sheets, transported? How long will they last? What is the quality? Do they need ironing? What works best for my guests? Such business decisions "are ongoing, and we challenge each other," says husband Steve, who has a master's degree in sustainable community development.

The couple operate the Pinehurst Inn, a bed-and-breakfast made of sandstone, maple and pine wood. It routinely tops Travel Green Wisconsin's listing of environmentally astute businesses. The inn is on the outskirts of Bayfield, a community known as one of the state's greenest destinations. Bayfield is a "special place because people take the time to take care of it," says Nancy.

Eight rooms are for rent, including three in a Garden House addition, which also has rooms big enough for meetings and retreats. There is a sauna, and the property has hiking trails. Locally grown food dominates the breakfast menu.

When Nancy and Steve bought the property, an 1885 country estate, it needed a lot of work. Among the environmentally friendly materials they selected for the renovation were solar panels to heat water, which paid for themselves "in a relatively short period of time." Most rooms have whirlpool baths but, they say, "we are very tuned in to our water usage, and have a state-of-the-art septic system."

The Sandstroms' daughter Darcy Schwerin and her husband, Michael, operate the on-site **Enso Wellness and Day Spa**, offering yoga classes, massage treatments, and other wellness services.

Pinehurst Inn at Pike's Creek
83645 Highway 13
Bayfield, Wisconsin
www.pinehurstinn.com 877-499-7651
•

The sauna is the perfect place to relax after a hike or bike ride.

WISCONSIN

Amish and "English" watch the auction action.

GROWERS PRODUCE AUCTION

Cashton, Wisconsin

"Let's go fifty, a dollar-fifty. Now two. And fifty. Now three. And fifty, just fifty—do we have three-fifty? Fifty?

"Sold, for three dollars. All right, times forty-five . . ."

Yikes! Had I just bought 45 double-impatiens for $135? Or did he say "four or five"?

Neither. Auctioneer Philip Wolf was just rushing into his next sing-song of bids, for flats of smaller flowers. My purchase was "times 12"—which means I bought a dozen near-identical plants. The foot-tall flowers were lush, fat with blossoms.

The lyrical, rhythmic chants of the auctioneers are the kind of serenade that could rival rap musicians. The lilt seems hypnotic, and this is a part of what turns a sale into an event.

Amish families in southwest Wisconsin sell their products at least twice weekly during summer at the Growers Produce Auction, but the Memorial Day and Labor Day sales are by far the biggest.

The sale of thousands of potted flowers and/or vegetables, about 100 handcrafted quilts, numerous pieces of hand-carved furniture and other crafts keep three sets of auctioneers busy from 8:30 a.m. to 4:30 p.m. on the two holidays. Hundreds of handmade baskets and rugs are sold per auction. As harvests ripen, there will be fewer plants in pots and more freshly picked produce.

At the other auctions, product selection all fits into the auction house and is sold by one auctioneer (who actually was German Baptist, not Amish). A few of the 150 consigners are "English" (non-Amish). Typical customers are wholesalers who buy merchandise in large quantities, although items in smaller amounts also are sold. Most growers live within a 100-mile radius of Cashton. When products are sold from farther away, they are identified as such before bidding begins.

Sometimes finished quilts or quilt tops come from as far away as Pennsylvania and fetch up to $700. The buyer of a quilt top, to which a back and batting must be added, has the option of hiring a local Amish woman to finish the project.

The auction house helps the Amish obtain supplies that might otherwise be out of their reach. That includes cardboard tote boxes to hold ten pounds of asparagus, or the plastic planters that become flourishing flower arrangements through greenhouse gardening.

A part of the auction allure is the appealing mix of merchandise and the ease with which customers can get swept into the bidding process. Getting a bargain means knowing your bottom line—and how much you're buying—before bidding begins.

Not all auctioneers operate alike, and that can be confusing. One auctioneer may let a winning bidder take only as many of an item as is desired. Another will hold the top bidder responsible for an entire lot of merchandise. The rules tend to be clear, but explanations are quick.

It's fun to simply watch the action and people. Or arrive with friends and make bidding decisions as a group. Or be aware when strangers buy more than expected. So when an auctioneer declared a winning bid of $17.50 for gorgeous hanging baskets, and the buyer flashed the peace sign, we smelled opportunity.

"That was times four," the top bidder was told, with no room for negotiation, because a new sale began. We made a beeline her way, struck a private deal and soon took two baskets off her hands.

Growers Produce Auction
S347 Dell Road
Cashton, Wisconsin
608-654-7880
•

Northwestern Wisconsin's Totogatic Flowage

DOWN TO EARTH TOURS

Gordon, Wisconsin

Dave Thorson stops his 14-passenger bus and takes out a pouch of tobacco. He talks about a ritual that goes back thousands of years. We are at the wild and unblemished Totogatic Flowage in northwest Sawyer County, and Dave tosses bits of tobacco in four directions, as an offering to the Great Spirit and ancestors of this land.

For seven hours, we learn about the way life used to be in this part of northwest Wisconsin, when the Ojibwe were caretakers of the land and every full moon was a time of thanksgiving—for strawberries in June, or wild rice in September.

"After a history lesson on Indian culture in fourth grade, we don't get much of this information as adults," our guide observes. "We've kind of lost our connection to Mother Earth."

He drives almost 100 miles as we traverse little-known wonders of Sawyer, Douglas and Bayfield counties. The First American Cultural Tour is a part of Down to Earth Tours, a business that Dave began in 2006.

Some of the tour is on land owned by Dave or his parents. "My Grandpa Louie said he fished every trout hole in this area. He's the kind of guy who would say, 'You ever been down that road, David? Let's see where it goes.' A little of that spirit lives on in me."

Dave has a forestry degree from the University of Minnesota. He worked in Idaho as a seasonal firefighter, in forestry/hydrology and wildlife/fisheries jobs, and moved back to develop an environmental education curriculum for Wisconsin schools. "Teaching has been in my blood," he says. "I love to share what I know with others."

We loop around Ounce, Upper St. Croix and White River watersheds, bounce from paved to dirt roads, learn about a nineteenth-century maple sugar camp and wild rice patches on deserted Lake Pacwawong, a once-vibrant Native American village.

We walk hunched over to enter an abandoned copper mine and see four-foot muskies at a hand-operated lock and dam in the town of Barnes.

Dave uses essays and maps dating back to the 1700s to explain local history and heritage. We hear music and prose. We sniff trailing arbutus—"the first flower you'll see here as winter ends"—inspect wolf scat, see where the world's largest musky was caught and talk about bird sounds, burial mounds, Clovis to Woodland artifacts.

His lessons change with the seasons. The area is home to bobcats, badgers and western fox snakes, but today we only catch a glimpse of two whitetails.

Down to Earth Tours are a mix of ecology, geology, history and culture. Excursions are scheduled from Earth Day to mid-November.

In our group are retired teachers and hardcore conservationists, including a lifelong forager and Ice Age Trail leaders. What results is a conversation, not a lecture, with a dozen stops relevant to the day's theme.

"We know more about the Indians of South America than we do our own neighbors," Dave says. "I'm on their side—they got a raw deal on everything, but I think the way to handle it is with awareness, not by hiding the culture away."

Down to Earth Tours
Gordon, Wisconsin
www.downtoearthtours.com 715-376-4260
•

WISCONSIN

Dairy farmer Nick Engelbert created art obsessively.

GRANDVIEW

Hollandale, Wisconsin

"Think like Nick," the teacher advises her students.

More than 200 children bring their treasures and stories to school in May, then begin walking—one mile west, all uphill—to give up the material goods and cement the memories.

"If we don't get rained out, it's a wonderful event," says Marilyn Rolfsmeyer, a K–12 art teacher in the Argyle School District.

The Great Grandview Parade occurs in Iowa County's Hollandale, population 300. The annual trek begins at the elementary school and ends at Nick Engelbert's Grandview, a spectacular and unusual art environment on Highway 39, between New Glarus and Mineral Point.

No one else in the world possesses a precious but rough jewel quite like Grandview, named that by Nick because of the peaceful and pretty landscape that surrounds his homestead.

A dairy farmer who died in 1962, Nick spent 30 years lovingly and obsessively creating concrete sculptures of elves, peacocks and other creatures throughout his yard and home. All are embellished with stones, shells, colorful glass bits and throwaway materials.

No one knows if the adornments are simply scraps of trash or more. Look closely, and you'll occasionally see something more personal than broken bottles, lightning rod insulators and shards of unidentifiable origin.

Are remnants of porcelain figurines, for example, in the mix on purpose or by accident? That's where the exercise for children comes in, when they add personal items to a wall of a storage shed, built on Grandview in 2001.

"They leave a piece of their own history, their own time capsule," embedded in wet cement, Marilyn explains. "They each bring one thing to immortalize" their lives. "When you are old and gray, what would you want others to see as a reminder of you?" she asks her students. "You'd be surprised by what they bring, and the stories." It could be a piece of Grandma's jewelry, or a cherished little toy. Marilyn's own contribution was a baby spoon, one that fed all three of her children.

Nick's Grandview was inspired by his visit to the garish but glistening Dickeyville Grotto, an art environment of similar spirit, at Holy Ghost Catholic Church, 50 miles southwest of Hollandale.

Both sites are manmade shrines of self-expression, produced by people with no formal art training. Wisconsin is a global leader in the identification and preservation of such projects, also known as outsider art.

Who says? Several people, including Iain Jackson, an architecture professor at the University of Liverpool in England. He and other art specialists have traveled to Wisconsin for an international conference on outsider art.

Why Wisconsin? The Kohler Foundation in the late 1970s spearheaded efforts to identify, protect and preserve these environments, then make them accessible to the public. The Pecatonica Educational Charitable Foundation, after help from the Kohler Foundation, owns and maintains Grandview. Grounds are open until dark daily. The museum (once Nick's home) is open by appointment and usually on Tuesday through Sunday, between Memorial Day and Labor Day. Admission is free, but donations are appreciated.

Grandview
7351 Highway 39
Hollandale, Wisconsin
www.nicksgrandview.com 608-967-2151
•

Other sites preserved by the Kohler Foundation:

Drifter Ernest Hupeden's **Painted Forest**, Highway EE, Valton
•

Farmer-logger Fred Smith's **Wisconsin Concrete Park**, Highway 100, Phillips
•

Farmer Herman Rusch's **Prairie Moon Sculpture Garden**, Highway 35, between Fountain City and Cochrane
•

Furniture detailer **James Tellen Woodland Sculpture Garden**, Evergreen Drive, Black River Point
•

Paul and Matilda **Wegner Grotto** (also called the Glass Church), Highway 71, Cataract

Kohler Foundation
www.kohlerfoundation.org 920-458-1972
•

Don't miss these other examples of outsider art in Wisconsin:

Tom Every's **Dr. Evermor's Art Park**, Highway 12, Baraboo
•

Jurustic Park, off Highway E and north of Marshfield, a creation of Clyde and Nancy Wynia, retired lawyer and nurse
•

An inspiration for some of these artists was the **Dickeyville Grotto**, 305 W. Main Street, Dickeyville, adjacent to the Holy Ghost Church. www.dickeyvillegrotto.com 608-568-3119
•

It is the same with the **Rudolph Grotto Gardens and Wonder Cave**, adjacent to St. Philip Catholic Church, 6975 Grotto Avenue, Rudolph. www.rudolphgrotto.org 715-435-3286

Cormorants linger in Horicon Marsh.

HORICON MARSH BOAT TOURS
Horicon, Wisconsin

Farm families didn't take vacations when I was a kid. We took Sunday drives, leisurely ventures into the countryside to assess the corn and alfalfa. What we learned about nature's rhythms depended on the season.

The exception was our annual autumn pilgrimage to Horicon Marsh. The big attraction was Canada geese—not a V-shaped formation of mournful honkers, but one cornfield of birds after another, turning the fields a near-solid black.

We would skirt the 32,000-acre perimeter, following a 36-mile loop in Dodge and Fond du Lac counties that is known today as Horicon Marsh Parkway. Decades passed before I visited the area's ecological wealth during another season.

Hundreds of bird species—egrets and owls, mergansers and gnatcatchers—have long relied on this complex ecosystem, the nation's largest cattail marsh. A few birds (like the orange-beaked Forster's tern and the petite, elusive yellow rail) are labeled "endangered" or "threatened."

Few know this part of the world better than Marc Zuelsdorf. His Horicon Marsh Boat Tours visits this environmentally diverse swampland, which is one part state wildlife area and two parts national refuge. Marc's near-constant narration ("Look up—those dots are American White pelicans" and "See the heron standing in those reeds?") means even novice bird watchers can appreciate the tour.

Rent a canoe and paddle the marsh on several water trails.

Many of us on the 48-person pontoon boat bring binoculars to spot wildlife. Waterways narrow and bend, to reveal camouflaged life in feathered and furry forms. "What you see depends on many things," Marc says, matter-of-factly. "Time of day, time of year, type of weather."

A cluster of cormorants perches in trees that sway on a sliver of island. A great blue heron gives a low and throaty croak. The noisy tweets and twitters of myriad species are impossible for the untrained ear to separate. Not everything seen or heard can be identified.

We get close to a beaver lodge and watch a woodchuck swim. We tally 40 species of birds in two hours; 300 species have been documented here. We hear an uncommon American bittern, whose booming voice is easier to identify than its earth-toned coat of feathers. "It's a surprise every time you're out there," Marc says.

The annual Horicon Marsh Bird Festival in early May guarantees eye-to-eye contact with hawks, eagles or kestrels, when a wildlife rehabilitation specialist talks about her work and astounds her audience with one predator after another taken from cloth-covered cages.

The Canada goose might be what draws bird lovers to Horicon for the first time, but the diversity is what brings me back for more.

Horicon Marsh Boat Tours conducts narrated marsh trips of one hour or longer, May 1 to October 25. Canoes and kayaks are for rent.

Two-thirds of Horicon Marsh is federally protected. Some hiking trails and observation decks are usable all year.

Horicon Marsh Boat Tours
311B Mill Street
Horicon, Wisconsin
www.horiconmarsh.com 920-485-4663

•

Preregister for **Horicon Marsh Bird Festival** events when fees are involved, particularly sunrise and twilight birding tours, and all-day bus-boat outings. www.horiconmarshbirdfestival.com 920-485-2936

•

Check out interpretive programs, exhibits and lectures at the **Horicon Marsh International Education Center**, N7725 Highway 28, Horicon. www.horiconmarsh.org 920-387-7860

•

Events also sometimes are arranged at **Horicon Marsh State Wildlife Area**. www.dnr.wi.gov 920-387-7860

•

Hiking and bicycling on the Old Marsh Road of **Horicon National Wildlife Refuge** are limited to daylight hours on summer weekends. www.fws.gov/midwest/horicon 920-387-2658

Can you spot the great blue heron?

The building addition respects the principles of Frank Lloyd Wright's work.

FIRST UNITARIAN SOCIETY

Madison, Wisconsin

Frank Lloyd Wright was among the early members of Madison's First Unitarian Society, whose original Meeting House was designed by the architect and completed in 1951.

By 2000, the Society had outgrown the church, and members discussed whether to expand or relocate. The congregation decided on expansion,

A GREEN GUIDE FOR TRAVELERS   149

Rain percolates through the gravel, and sedum grows on the roof.

but also hastened work to ensure the integrity, preservation and future of the original structure, designated a National Historic Landmark.

The new building is LEED-certified at the gold level because the congregation kept as its priorities Wright's love of organic architecture—structural design that respects nature—and the desire to be authentically sustainable.

Plants fill the roof. Low-flush toilets save water. Geothermal heating and cooling systems cut energy costs. Huge windows lessen the need for artificial lighting. Everything—from ventilation systems to dish washing practices—involves green design. The original Meeting House in 1960 was deemed one of 17 structures that exemplify Wright's contribution to American culture. The designation came from the American Institute of Architects.

The project stands as an example of the congregation's desire to practice what it preaches—environmental stewardship—without compromising structural heritage.

First Unitarian Society is among the largest Unitarian-Universalist congregations in the world. Tours occur daily from May through October, and all year on Sundays after worship services.

First Unitarian Society
900 University Bay Drive
Madison, Wisconsin
www.fusmadison.org 608-233-9774

•

Monona Terrace as seen from Lake Monona

WISCONSIN

Another must-see for Frank Lloyd Wright fans:

Monona Terrace Community and Convention Center, 1 John Nolen Drive, Madison. Designed by Wright in 1938 but not realized until 1997, the conspicuous white edifice on Lake Monona is a popular public gathering space because of its generous lake views. The rooftop garden is the site of free concerts in summer. Musical performances move indoors during colder months. Building tours daily. Grand View Cafe open Monday through Saturday, 7:30 a.m. to 2:30 p.m.

www.mononaterrace.com 608-261-4000

Locavores find friendly and inventive dining at Graze.

GRAZE

Madison, Wisconsin

Chef Tory Miller buys not steaks and chops but whole cows and pigs from local farms, using as much of the animals as possible in his fine dining menus.

Such practices are not uncommon for a well-trained chef who truly wants to lessen unnecessary waste while supporting the work of local farmers. Tory is among the best in Wisconsin who do this, and in 2010 his business location, scope and audience expanded dramatically.

His restaurant, L'Etoile, moved less than one block and expanded about 100 percent in capacity, 75 percent in physical size. To the left of the main entrance: fine dining. To the right: a new dimension, Graze, a casual gastropub that serves locally grown food, some presented in unconventional ways.

Tory classifies the gastropub menu as "modern American comfort food." He'll serve pastrami, made with beef tongue, and roasted bone marrow, teamed with pickled shallots.

The chef sees nothing wrong with a traditional Friday fish fry, but his version involves "sustainable sourcing, perfectly cooked" with "a vodka batter, not beer, because the liquid evaporates faster, so the batter gets super crisp and thin." Add a tartar sauce with from-scratch mayo, plus capers and fresh herbs— "a familiar taste, but with something extra."

The approach, Tory believes, fills a void because mainstream restaurant meals with truly local, sustainable ingredients are rare. "If I want to go out and have fried chicken, the options aren't there," he says. "I like to cook with other cooks in mind," which also means offering eclectic choices—from oysters and patés to burgers and hot wings—with unconventional spins.

Consider meatballs of ground rabbit or chicken, with ground pine nuts instead of breadcrumbs as the binder. A quick lunch might mean Reuben sandwiches "made with our own corned beef and rye bread."

Odessa Piper, a pioneer in the "go-local" movement, established L'Etoile in 1976. By 2001, she had earned Best Chef in the Midwest honors from the James Beard Foundation. "The new L'Etoile team keeps busting out with new takes on the local food scene, so this step just seems like a natural fit for their passion and creativity," she says, of her successors' expansion.

Tory, sister Traci Miller and Dianne Christensen are co-owners of Graze and L'Etoile.

Tory was invited to cook Thanksgiving dinner at Manhattan's James Beard House in 2006, the same year *Gourmet* magazine ranked L'Etoile as one of America's top 50 restaurants. In 2008 L'Etoile made *Saveur* magazine's list of top 100 restaurants.

The chef says much of the business expansion is about walking the talk: "If opening a second restaurant in a casual style makes it easier for more people to eat local, sustainable food, then that's a good thing."

L'Etoile

Graze

1 S. Pinckney Street

Madison, Wisconsin

www.letoile-restaurant.com 608-251-0500

www.grazepub.com 608-251-2700

•

WISCONSIN

Other food innovators are turning up nearby, on and off Capitol Square:

Merchant, 121 S. Pinckney Street, is Madison's first urban grocery-restaurant combo, with a craft cocktail bar and "gourmet-to-go" food option. The kitchen mastermind is Brian Hauke, former executive chef at the Red Stag Supper Club, Minneapolis, which was Minnesota's first LEED-certified restaurant.

"The urban grocery is the kitchen's pantry," full of ingredients that go into the restaurant's meals, says Merchant, on Facebook. "Shoppers may actually find themselves selecting their fresh greens right next to a member of Merchant's kitchen team."

So, it's artisan breads and cheeses to organic meats and poultry. Veggies grown by local Hmong residents and organic cheese made by the bucket on Amish farms are on Merchant's radar.

www.merchantmadison.com 608-259-9799

•

"Big things to come," announced **Underground Food Collective Kitchen**, 127 E. Mifflin Street, Madison, upon being issued a meat processing license in 2010. Brothers Jonny and Ben Hunter believe in going whole hog, literally.

The license means they can make their own sausages, cure their own meats and teach others to do the same.

The renegade chefs—who began as caterers but didn't want to be locked into a menu or made to wear uniforms—in 2010 opened their off-the-Square business as a dinner and late-night restaurant. Next step: hands-on cooking and butchering classes.

They considered not having a menu, and instead just asking customers a few basic questions about food preferences, then surprising them. Maybe later. First come the basics, and that means getting people accustomed to the complete local bounty of whatever the season.

"Seasonal Wisconsin cuisine is almost a style now," Jonny says, because local farmers' products are becoming better known. UFC tries to limit its key ingredients to what is sold in the Upper Midwest.

Some meals, like pork roast, are priced at single portions. Other items, such as the vegetable, cheese and meat boards are meant for sharing.

And the cocktail list? It's another seasonal affair—"Classic cocktails, but with a Wisconsin twist," says Jonny—which means a backbone of close-to-home beverages, plus concoctions that the Hunters make with local ingredients. The latter even includes bitters; their version requires the steeping of peach seeds (found inside the pit) and a mix of herbs (thyme, allspice and more) in a beet and sugar alcohol for at least four months.

Add the bitters to a combination of Death's Door vodka and grapefruit juice, on ice. Or, for a lighter version of a Bloody Mary, combine herb-infused vodka, tomato water and a pickled tomatillo. Do these drinks have fancy names? Hah! Each simply gets a number. This place does not play by conventional rules.

The endeavor balances typical and adventurous fare. Think pot roast vs. rabbit hearts. Down-home flavors vs. influences from Jonny's travels in Spain, Argentina, France and Germany.

A food class might involve organ meats or pig blood, and we can talk about the traditions where these things come from.

What's the old saying? When the student is ready, the teacher appears. First, the family-style pot roast and seasonal cocktails.

The Hunters also are key advocates of the annual Bike the Barns (www.macsac.org/bikethebarns), a September fundraiser for community-supported agriculture that involves visits (and eating) at Wisconsin farms.

wwww.undergroundfoodcollective.org 608-514-1516

Underground chef Ben Hunter likes to shake up the status quo.

Look for the log cabin and live chickens on the museum roof.

MADISON CHILDREN'S MUSEUM

Madison, Wisconsin

The Madison Children's Museum tripled its size in 2010 by moving to a new location, a former Montgomery Ward department store built in 1929. Exhibits get children moving and learning.

Homing pigeons and chickens live on the fifth-floor rooftop, as do a vegetable garden, fish and a honey locust tree. The "park in the sky"—open all year—also contains a greenhouse, waterfall, wind turbine (made of bicycle parts) and prime views of the State Capitol and Lake Mendota.

An 1838 log cabin was moved to the museum parking lot from Walworth County and restored. Inside are household items from the era that teach history as kids churn butter, write with a quill pen and learn about herbal medicines.

The Wildernest introduces preschoolers to other cultures, through play in themed huts. Children also can walk a suspended bridge (which resembles a set of ribs) and maneuver a horizontal climbing wall (not taller than most parents).

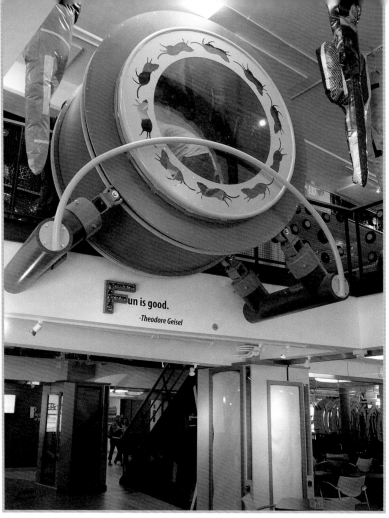

It's no rat race, but it sure is fun at the Madison Children's Museum.

WISCONSIN

A big-as-life cow model sits atop a roof. Another hangs from a ceiling harness and moves through a counterbalancing of milk cans and toy cheese wedges.

Affixed to museum walls are bottlecaps, each containing a piece of art from 13,000 schoolchildren, then filled with resin to preserve the art and smooth the surface.

The work of 100 artists is scattered throughout the museum. On the roof are a 3,400-pound bird with two heads and a cheese-kettle body, made with salvaged materials by Tom "Dr. Evermor" Every of Baraboo. Steps away is a mural dome of Wisconsin scenes by Richard Haas of Spring Green, transplanted from a condo project.

What else? A model railroading club donated and installed a $30,000 train set that chugs and loops overhead. Volunteers sewed recycled material into dozens of felted animals, a substitute for plastic toys.

The $16.5 million museum project hopes to be a nationwide leader in sustainable business practices and design, in part for its use of reclaimed and donated materials and décor.

Wood from a collapsed barn turns into a "squashed house" under a stairwell. Slats from a junior high school's old wooden basketball court are rearranged and installed as artsy floorboard. Each bathroom stall is made of 1,600 recycled milk containers. Old road signs and board games are transformed into seats and tabletops.

"We're eager to use this building as a teaching tool for sustainable living" and to help children learn lifelong habits, says Ruth Shelly, the museum's executive director. Children can go on a "green scavenger hunt" inside the museum. "Our ideas came from all over the world," Ruth says, but most building materials are from within 100 miles of Madison.

The museum's "solar chicken" (not to be confused with the live ones on the roof) will "produce" a golden egg for every kilowatt of power that rooftop solar panels produce.

The museum received national recognition—a Promising Practice Award, which rewards eco efforts—from the MetLife Foundation and Association of Children's Museums. In 2011 it was rated among the top five children's museums in the country.

Madison Children's Museum
100 N. Hamilton Street
Madison, Wisconsin
www.madisonchildrensmuseum.org 608-256-6445
•

The kids' menu rules at **Bean Sprouts** (inside the Madison Children's Museum), and it's all about enticing children to eat healthful food. Clever names and fun food presentations help to make this happen. Example: The type of sauce (marinara vs. cheese) and shape of whole wheat pasta (ravioli vs. macaroni) are what distinguish Noodle-Dee-DOO and Noodle-Dee-DEE on the menu.

Owners Shannon Payette Seip and Kelly Parthen wrote *Bean Appetit: Hip and Healthy Ways to Have Fun with Food.*

www.beansproutscafe.com 608-826-6YUM
•

*Anyone is welcome to tour this LEED platinum-certified building
and stroll the restored prairies surrounding the monastery.*

HOLY WISDOM MONASTERY

Middleton, Wisconsin

Work. Pray. Listen. Be aware. Welcome others. Use only what you need.

This—briefly stated—is the Rule of Benedict, which is at the heart of life at Holy Wisdom Monastery.

Years before LEED benchmarks were established, Holy Wisdom Monastery (then known as St. Benedict Center, the nation's first ecumenical Benedictine community for women) was tireless in its efforts to make environmental stewardship a priority. Prairie and wetland restoration brought 80 acres to its natural state and removed 85,000 cubic yards of silt from a 10,000-year-old glacial lake.

In planning a new building, Holy Wisdom chose a simple and uncluttered design—half the size of the building it replaced—that works in harmony with nature. In 2010 the U.S. Building Council recognized the building with a platinum rating, the highest level of LEED certification. As the nuns explained their work and philosophy to the council, "We strive to use only what we need, so resources can be preserved for others."

The view is stunning, as many others have noticed, including property developers who have proposed handsome offers to purchase the land. The nuns have declined. A golf course and lavish homes dominate adjacent property.

Everyone is welcome at Holy Wisdom, no matter their religion or lack of it. People come to rejuvenate or arrange confidential spiritual guidance. Accommodations range from simple guest bedrooms to private hermitages— little houses that overlook wooded areas. Some visitors come for worship services or community prayer. The monastery offers structure through events, and these include work on the woods or native prairie. The emphasis is on what makes people alike, not different.

Guided tours of the property are provided monthly. Self-guided tours are possible on weekdays from 8 a.m. to 4:30 p.m.

Holy Wisdom Monastery
4200 Highway M
Middleton, Wisconsin
www.benedictinewomen.org 608-836-1631
•

WISCONSIN

BRAISE ON THE GO
Milwaukee, Wisconsin

I always wanted to learn to hunt the elusive morel, yet never expected the hunt to coincide with a cooking class.

But that's the way it goes with Dave Swanson of Milwaukee, whose Braise on the Go routinely takes the kitchen and classroom on the road. The thrill of the hunt, during midspring, consists of slow walks through forests in search of rotting wood, dead elms in particular.

The winner's trophy carries great bragging rights and value, weighing in at three dollars or more per ounce. The hunter's weapon of choice is a sharp pocketknife, accompanied by keen eyesight and persistent, patient stalking.

"Our goal is to reconnect people with their food," Dave says.

This time, his 30 students met near woods for two-hour lessons in foraging, then nibbles of morels, ramps (wild garlic) and sorrel (resembling spinach) that Dave had turned into a light lunch, served from a portable food prep area in a parking lot.

The morel hunters I know never share their hunting spots, not even with their best friend.

In Dave's crowd were first-time hunters and two-generation veteran teams, guided by fungi fanatics from as far away as Washington's Puget Sound. I stuck close to Britt Bunyard, publisher and editor of *Fungi* magazine (www.fungimag.com); he has a doctorate in plant pathology and a master's degree in botany.

So this was no lightweight support team, but I can't say we sniffed out a yeoman's harvest of morels. What we did was learn a lot about what grows in the wild.

Dave chops wild-caught ramps and morels.

WISCONSIN

Britt pointed out a patch of elms, oaks and grasses. "Good for chanterelles," he explained; the yellow-orange fungi should pop up in mid-July to mid-August.

We inspected new, bulbous growth on a poplar tree. "Oyster mushrooms," he noted. "A little early in the season, and small, but we'll take them, so everybody else can see."

Dave chopped and sautéed ramps with morels, then scooped them atop crostini spread with brandy-spiked paté of lamb livers.

"He's got some serious cooking skills," Britt says, and no one in the crowd would disagree. A former chef de cuisine at Milwaukee's Sanford restaurant, Dave attended Le Cordon Bleu in Paris after graduating from Kendall College School of Culinary Arts in Chicago.

He is a deliberate champion of locally grown food, and he makes connections in unconventional ways. It is not unusual for him to pack up and head to a farm, a botanical garden or—yes—a forest for a cooking class. "The idea is to see where food comes from" and better understand "all the little edibles out there," he explained.

Another branch of his business: restaurant-supported agriculture (RSA), similar in spirit to the community-supported agriculture (CSA) shares that individuals purchase, to support the work of family farms. RSAs and CSAs share the risk of farming, through at least partial prepayment for a portion of the harvest.

Dave's network involves 15 restaurants and at least 40 farms per season. Instead of having farmers make deliveries to several restaurants, there is one drop-off point, which makes the RSA concept different from initiatives that simply make it easier for farmers and chefs to meet. "It's a daunting task," he says of the work, to match supply and demand, but worth the effort.

Braise on the Go
www.braiseculinaryschool.com
414-241-9577
•

The tour company **Learn Great Foods** conducts culinary farm tours in Michigan, Illinois, Wisconsin, Iowa, Missouri and Kentucky. Day trips and weekend retreats to specialty shops and agricultural locations give participants an opportunity to chat with food producers. A guest chef teaches while preparing a meal of fresh foods and products of that site. Itineraries can be customized for private groups.

www.learngreatfoods.com 866-240-1650
•

See dancing and more at Milwaukee's annual Indian Summer Festival.

INDIAN SUMMER FESTIVAL

Milwaukee, Wisconsin

For Native Americans, harvests are about gratitude, sustenance and preserving a way of life. Consider wild rice, which has a place at special occasions, from funerals to celebrations. Even the harvest, done by hand, is a sacred act.

Some rice is tapped off of reeds, falling into the wetlands, to help the rice bed reseed itself. Additional rice is deliberately left for wildlife. The attitude is one of sustainability and responsibility to the well-being of many species, now and among future generations.

Wild rice is part of the annual Indian Summer Festival on Milwaukee's lakefront. The fest celebrates the diversity of Native American culture in Wisconsin. Wild rice rituals are but one aspect of Indian culture, and this festival, held in early September, widens the classroom to include everyone.

Traditional skills, from weaving to beadwork, are demonstrated. So is dancing in native dress and the teaching of tribal lore through storytelling. Particularly dramatic are the Sunday prayer service and the intertribal, multigenerational powwows. "Festive and sacred" is how festival organizers aptly describe the experience, which includes replicas of authentic tribal villages and dozens of vendors, who sell handcrafted jewelry, herbal health remedies and much more.

Food vendors include Frybread Express, Spring Creek Bison, Turkey Tee Pee and Whitefeather. Look for wild rice in soups and casseroles and sold uncooked by the pound. Hull corn soup, buffalo jerky, venison brats and walleye filet sandwiches are other choices.

Omnipresent frybread—puffy and sometimes slightly sweet—works as a dessert (with cinnamon sugar), holds a meal (like a sandwich) and suffices as a dip for sauces (like a tortilla). It is best when eaten freshly fried. The addition of beans, meat and cheese, served open-face, turns the bread into Indian tacos.

Frybread has Navajo roots, although many other tribes have adopted it as their own. It was a symbol of survival and captivity in the 1800s, when Native Americans were forced onto reservations. Tribes invented it as a way to use the meager government rations of powdered milk, baking powder, lard, flour, salt and sugar.

It's one thing to witness Native American rituals and another to partici-pate. Wisconsin's **Oneida Nation** encourages adults and children to assist with the early autumn harvesting of five acres of corn on the tribe's 83-acre organic farm at 139 Riverdale Drive, Oneida.

The annual **Harvest and Husking Bee** is about straightforward work more than symbolic rituals, says Ted Skenandore, the Oneida's agriculture supervisor. "Heritage is a part of it, but hand harvesting is the best way for the corn to dry down because of its moisture content," he says. Husks are hand-braided, then added to long strings of many cobs and hung from barn rafters, so the corn doesn't mold.

The crop is white flint heirloom corn, brought by Oneida families when they moved to Wisconsin from New York in 1821. "We do our own seed saving before the harvest begins," Ted says. "This corn goes back to our creation story, which means before the beginning of time."

The harvest used to involve more pageantry, he says, but it wasn't practi-cal because "our corn would still be in the field after the party was over."

The corn is consumed in various ways: eaten raw, dehydrated, ground into flour, processed into soup, baked into bread, blended into a fresh berry mush (like an oatmeal). More than one dozen corn products and other organic products are sold at the small Tsyunhehkwa retail store in Ridgeview Plaza, 3759 W. Mason Street, Oneida.

Corn harvest helpers get lunch and a chance to win door prizes. Dates depend on the rhythms of the growing season.

www.oneidanation.org
920-869-2718
•

*Heirloom corn products for sale
at Tsyunhehkwa store*

WISCONSIN

Russ knows his audience and his beer.

LAKEFRONT BREWERY
Milwaukee, Wisconsin

Russ Klisch decided to ferment beer after brother Jim gave home-brewing a try. "It wasn't the worst beer I ever had," Russ deadpans, but he figured he could do it better.

That was 1982, and Russ (schooled as a chemist) today operates an unconventional laboratory in a former Cream City brick power plant. His Lakefront Brewery—the oldest certified organic brewery in the nation—makes award-winning craft beer in an ecologically thoughtful manner.

Lakefront products have made history. Its Organic ESB, out since 1996, was the nation's first certified organic beer. Ten years later, New Grist appeared as the first gluten-free beer. Local Acre was the first beer made with Wisconsin-grown hops and barley.

"We are the next wave of growth for breweries," Russ believes. Milwaukee brewers in the 1800s were very innovative, and Lakefront Brewery intends to uphold the spirit of this historic tradition.

Creativity extends beyond beer formulas. "We do things differently, like giving you a beer *before* a tour starts," Russ says. Guides—who include Jim Klisch, a retired police detective—joke around while explaining the brewing process.

What makes the brewery a leader environmentally?

- Every week, 15,000 pounds of the grain residue from brewing goes to Growing Power Inc., a Milwaukee nonprofit that specializes in urban gardening and bringing healthful food to all income levels. Growing Power uses worms to turn the spent grain into nutrient-rich compost.

- The brewery's home since 1998 is a refurbished 1908 coal-fired power plant on the Milwaukee River. The first location was a former bakery, where the brothers made beer in reconditioned dairy equipment.

- A portion of the brewery's energy comes from wind power. Water in a heat exchanger that cools wort (the liquid extracted in the mashing process during brewing) is reused.

- The brewery works with the Michael Fields Agricultural Institute to revive and support hops as a Wisconsin farm crop.

Visit Lakefront Brewery on a Friday night, and you can add supper and song to the experience. That's when a big room of the cavernous building is devoted to polka music and a longstanding Wisconsin tradition: the fish fry. The mood is boisterous, the setting family friendly and the beer ice cold.

The brewery also makes Lakefront Golden Maple Root Beer, which requires Wisconsin maple syrup but does not taste as syrupy as traditional root beers.

Lakefront Brewery
1872 N. Commerce Street
Milwaukee, Wisconsin
www.lakefrontbrewery.com 414-372-8800
•

More green places to visit in Milwaukee:

Absinthe used to be outlawed, but not anymore, and it's made at **Great Lakes Distillery**, 616 W. Virginia Street, which calls itself Wisconsin's first distillery since Prohibition. Tours occur on Fridays and Saturdays; a tasting/sales room is open more often. The small-batch business also produces a smooth, gently flavored line of vodkas and gins, which are international award winners and use Wisconsin products. One example: Roaring Dan's Rum contains a hint of pure maple syrup.

www.greatlakesdistillery.com 414-431-8683
•

WISCONSIN

Will Allen has been known to show up at potlucks with cartons full of greens, even in winter. The lettuce comes from **Growing Power**, 5500 W. Silver Spring Drive, which Will founded in 1993. The goal of this nonprofit organization is a simple one: "to grow food, to grow minds and to grow community."

People of many walks and ages have learned to grow fresh and healthful food in small, urban spaces because of Will's work, and his projects and training methods are used around the country. In 2010, he was one of *Time* magazine's 100 most influential people in the world.

Daily, 90-minute tours of Milwaukee's Growing Power include the gardens, honeybee hives, fish fertilizing plants and vermicompost areas (worm farms). Tours of Growing Power's work in Chicago are seasonal. Group reservations are required.

www.growingpower.org 414-527-1546

•

The LEED gold-certified Dorothy K. Vallier Environmental Learning Center is at the **Schlitz Audubon Nature Center**, 1111 E. Brown Deer Road. The center has 185 acres along Lake Michigan and is a 15-minute drive from downtown.

www.sanc.org 414-352-2880

Festive packaging at Great Lakes Distillery

Art photomurals feature Milwaukee women in sultry poses.

IRON HORSE HOTEL

Milwaukee, Wisconsin

The first time I met Milwaukee developer Tim Dixon, we wore hard hats and toured a gutted, musty, century-old warehouse near the Sixth Street viaduct in downtown Milwaukee. He was dreaming big and thinking impulsively, or so I thought.

His goal of creating a classy, one-of-a-kind and in-your-face hotel—a place to lounge with a cold beer or laptop, to hang your overcoat or leather jacket—seemed way over-the-top. I left with doubts.

Two weeks after Tim bought the building, Harley-Davidson announced that its $75 million museum would be constructed next door. Tim responded by buying a Harley and opening the Iron Horse, a sassy and stylish hotel unlike any other place that you're likely to spend the night. He emphasizes that it is built

Breakfast is served in Iron Horse's library.

for business execs in stiletto heels as well as dust-covered bikers: "It's comfortable here, like it was put together over time." He purchased many of the hotel's antique furnishings within one square mile of the hotel and has found ways to make industrial décor feel contemporary.

The hotel's amenities are most unusual: covered motorcycle parking, rag bins, check-in carts designed to move saddlebags, coat hooks sturdy enough to accommodate heavy leathers, on-site bike washing, service and rentals.

An enormous denim American flag, made out of 32.5 pairs of jeans, hangs on a brick lobby wall. In the 100 loft-style guest rooms is wall art that looks like poured foundry metal (one of many green features, because they are made from recycled aluminum).

Mural models are average women in mildly seductive poses, fashion photography by Milwaukee native Charles J. Dwyer that "challenges the stereotypes of Milwaukee women." Over the bigger-than-life images are hand-drawn embellishments, inspired by tattoo art. In-room bars are stocked with full-sized bottles of wine and premium liquors, plus cold beer. The property is dog friendly.

On the menu of Branded, the hotel bar, is a Slider Trio, miniburgers of kobe beef, pulled pork or veggies. The DLT adds duck confit to the traditional bacon-lettuce-tomato sandwich. During warm weather, drinks also are served outdoors in The Yard under colorful sails.

Smyth, the hotel restaurant, aims to mix comfort foods with artisan products and gourmet preparation. One example: Venison Osso Buco, a braised venison shank served with saffron risotto and roasted carrots.

Iron Horse Hotel
500 W. Florida Street
Milwaukee, Wisconsin
www.theironhorsehotel.com 888-543-4766
•

WISCONSIN

THE STONE BARN

Nelson, Wisconsin

"Build it, and they will come," I think, while climbing the hilly roads that dance with the creeks and curves of northwest Buffalo County. They come from neighboring farms and as far away as China, but are most likely to head here from Eau Claire, La Crosse and various Minnesota cities—Wabasha, Rochester, Minneapolis—just across the Mississippi.

Pizza rewards the adventurous traveler.

Hundreds come, past the cornfields and country cemeteries, some driving sporty convertibles and others paired up on motorcycles that whisk up, down and around this serene patch of the Driftless Area, where roads are more accustomed to slow-going tractors and thick-wheeled trucks.

Church Valley, German Valley, Norwegian Valley, Cascade Valley: Where you are depends upon your choice of route less traveled. No freeway quickly delivers you here.

The joy riders head to the Stone Barn on Friday, Saturday and Sunday nights from mid-May to mid-October. Pizzas with artisan meats and veggies—locally produced, when possible—slide into a 700-degree, wood-fired brick oven, but just for two minutes.

The pies come out with the thinnest and most pleasantly crisp crust possible, each piece barely sturdy enough to hold traditional to unconventional toppings. Expect a base of crushed tomatoes, not a sloppy sauce, or garlic olive oil instead of the tomatoes. Cheese? Maybe yes, maybe no.

WISCONSIN

It's a beautiful country setting and a perfect summer evening at the Stone Barn.

Consider the Alaskan: a spread of cream cheese, then smoked salmon, onion, dill and capers. Or the Greek, with feta cheese, spiced ground lamb, artichoke hearts, kalamata olives, onion and oregano.

Customers choose from eight combos (including the Muffaletta, patterned after a traditional New Orleans sandwich) or customize the toppings on their pies, which are priced from $18 to $23.

Couples typically make an evening out of eating these pizzas, then kick back with a cold beer or amble around the farmland, toward a backyard pond or through an antique shop on the premises. Some end the night with ice cream before heading home.

"People linger," says Pamela Taylor, co-owner with her husband, David Jacobs. "We light tiki torches, kids run around and it can get pretty loud."

By 5:30, a customer was carrying a number 30 tabletop sign from the ordering counter. It is not unusual for Pamela and David to make more than 100 pizzas in a night.

Pam bought this property because "I was driving around this area and loved it—even though the house was empty and the roof leaked so bad that a three-foot-thick icicle ran from floor to ceiling in the kitchen." Other than that, the farmhouse was sturdy and beautiful, full of natural woodwork and charm.

At the time, she was a computer systems analyst in the Twin Cities. "I wanted to do something I really loved, instead of what I was trained to do to make a living," she says. Today she makes noticeably less money but "I have everything—the views, the peace" and more freedom.

She arranged the removal of debris from a collapsed barn on the farm, but kept the structure's walls, built with stone quarried nearby. "I'll do something with this, someday," Pam promised herself, but "it kind of looked like Stonehenge for 15 years."

She had visited another "pizza farm," whose cook attracted more business than desired. "Why not try this," Pam thought, even though "some people thought I was nuts" because of the farm's remote location.

The barn walls turned into the guts of a building that could double as a greenhouse with an extension for shade plants, in case the pizza plan failed. As Pam explains it, "I like to grow things, and I like to cook."

The brick oven, a kitchen, customer seating and small bar (where Dave takes pizza orders) fill the greenhouse. Chalkboards list menu and beverage choices. Additional wrought iron tables and chairs dot an open-air patio, topped with a shade screen and flanked by columns of the barn stone.

Clusters of herbs grow thick in beds in this outdoor dining area, and Pam or her staff ("hard-working farm kids who live in the neighborhood") pick herbs for the pizzas, sometimes minutes before a night of business begins. Some of these seasonings also make their way into the locally raised pork and lamb that are ground for pizza toppings.

"I'm so thrilled that people feel comfortable here," Pam says, grinning as she works.

The Stone Barn
S685 Highway KK
Nelson, Wisconsin
www.nelsonstonebarn.com 715-673-4478
•

CEDAR GROVE CHEESE
Plain, Wisconsin

Wisconsin's excellence in cheesemaking turns into great bait for tourists, and about 70 of the state's 115 cheese factories accept visitors. A map from the Wisconsin Milk Marketing Board (www.eatwisconsincheese.com) outlines the trail of cheese all over the state.

Southwest Wisconsin is an especially rich cheese production area, and one plant has designed an earth-friendly way to deal with the wastewater that is part of cheese production.

The people at Cedar Grove Cheese in Plain believe it is environmentally important to purify wastewater—whey, spilled milk and soapy water used to clean milk trucks and cheese vats—instead of simply spreading it onto farmland as a fertilizer. To accomplish this, they designed the Living Machine, an ecosystem that handles about 7,000 gallons daily of wash water (from washing out the tanks of milk trucks and cheesemaking equipment), using microbes and hydroponic plants to clean the water naturally, then discharging it into Honey Creek.

The process takes up to four days to complete. First, bacteria break down residue as the water enters closed aerobic tanks. Then the water moves into tanks with plants whose roots in water "provide a new ecosystem for more diverse microbial populations." Solid residue settles, and much can be used as field fertilizer. Water, now clear, runs through filters before entering the neighborhood creek.

Tours of the Living Machine and cheese factory, which makes organic cheeses—including curds, herb-flavored cheddars, mixed-milk products—can be arranged. The company's award winners include Goat Milk Cheddar, Dante Lamb and Caprico (a goat-cow milk mix).

Cedar Grove Cheese
E5904 Mill Road
Plain, Wisconsin
www.cedargrovecheese.com
800-200-6020
•

Wastewater is cleaned and recycled in the Living Machine at Cedar Grove Cheese.

A great old brewery is resurrected near the Mississippi River.

NATIONAL BREWERY MUSEUM

Potosi, Wisconsin

The Great River Road, nearly 3,000 miles long, leads motorists through ten states along the Mississippi. One of the smaller towns on this national parkway made big-time history by opening a national museum.

Potosi, population 725 and in the southwest corner of Wisconsin, is home to the National Brewery Museum, a $6 million project that St. Louis and Milwaukee tried in vain to lure. The American Breweriana Association chose Potosi for its long brewing history and residents who would see the project through.

The museum occupies the four-story 1852 Potosi Brewing Company. "We're fortunate this building was still standing," says Frank Fiorenza, village president. "It looked war torn, but the foundation was still solid."

Also in the building is a Great River Road interpretive center, transportation (road, rail, river) museum, national brewery reference library, gift shop, microbrewery and restaurant.

The brewmaster taps into local spring water to produce seasonal brews: Princess Potosa (a root beer), Potosi Pure Malt Cave Ale (an amber ale), Good

Old Potosi (a pilsner) and Snake Hollow IPA (a reference to rattlesnakes found in area mining caves).

Sometimes the beer also shows up on the museum's restaurant menu. There's beer cheese soup with smoked gouda and roasted red peppers, and brats boiled in Cave Ale before grilled.

Vintage television beer ads play. Exhibit items come from hundreds of private collections. (Passage Thru Time, a longstanding Potosi history museum with Osceola arrowheads and artifacts, also has beer memorabilia.)

Expect to see rare, pre-Prohibition brewing equipment, long stored in a farm shed. Unusual tales revolve around the Potosi Steamer, which until 1917 delivered pony kegs to Dubuque, Iowa, while quenching the thirst of 100 passengers. "Potosi's rolling bar, for 30 years," Frank says. "It was the bar that came to you."

Then there was the elongated 1929 Pontiac—big enough for six bartenders to work out of at once and a popular rental unit for weddings. "It had no liquor license," Frank says, "so you couldn't sell beer from it, but you could give it away. We have so many artifacts, we can change exhibits easily during the year."

Ripley's Believe It or Not noticed Potosi in the 1940s and decided it had the longest Main Street without an intersection. The community is sandwiched between two bluffs. Main Street ends at the 240,000-acre Upper Mississippi River Refuge, a national wildlife area. Visitors also tour the 1827 St. John lead mine in Potosi, or take a tube float on the Grant River.

National Brewery Museum
209 S. Main Street
Potosi, Wisconsin
www.potosibrewery.com 608-763-4002
•

Many items in the museum were donated by Breweriana members.

WISCONSIN

A comfortable well-lit space is a great place to unwind.

WOODWIND HEALTH SPA

Rhinelander, Wisconsin

We are following the Wisconsin River, off of Highway 8, looking for a dirt road. It leads to a gray stucco building, but the sign says Not the Spa, so we veer right—our only option—and follow a couple more curves.

The journey ends and begins among the ash, poplar and evergreens, just west of Rhinelander and Nicolet National Forest. An estimated 250 lakes, rivers and streams are within a 15-minute drive.

When a spa is an overnight destination, most people don't expect a low-budget experience. This is an exception. The 42-acre Woodwind Health Spa has a Native American influence. *Budget Travel* magazine in 2006 chose Woodwind as one of the top 15 spa values nationwide.

Owner Marj Champney, of Pennacook tribal descent, considers this a place to change as well as unwind. "The word 'spa' helps to keep a roof over our heads and get people through the door," she says, "so the healing can begin."

Both sexes are welcome, and single travelers likely will feel at ease because the property has a communal energy. There are hiking trails and indoor nooks for private retreat. Accommodations for up to 24 people range from dorm beds to private rooms, and all are clean, cheerful and furnished simply. Bathrobes are provided for the hallway walk to bathrooms.

Rates include breakfast, and other meals can be purchased because Woodwind has a restaurant license.

A friend and I are the only overnight guests on a Thursday night and arrive in time for a late-day yoga class. Drumming, chanting and meditation sessions also can be arranged.

Then comes dinner, a fresh and balanced buffet, and my vegetarian companion and I both eat well. The $15 meal includes a glass of wine, plus table talk about what brings people together.

The next morning, we eat fresh fruit and organic granola while watching a half dozen deer eat leftover greens, tossed near the bird feeders. It all feels more like a B&B than a hotel, but without the Victorian frills.

There also are gift shops. One has crystals, oils, jewelry, aromatherapy products and self-improvement books.

Staff will host nondenominational retreats, organize workshops for cancer survivors, teach volunteers how to avoid burnout and welcome solo travelers or groups of friends who want to relax in a quiet and natural setting.

When I visit, unusual spa services include the $110 Eagle's Touch Massage, a 90- to 120-minute service that incorporates crystals, oils and heated stones. The $110 Raindrop Therapy combines massage, reflexology and cranial-sacral healing for up to 90 minutes.

Donations defray the expenses for women who could benefit from but can't afford the facility's services.

Woodwind Health Spa
3033 Woodwind Way
Rhinelander, Wisconsin
www.woodwindspa.com
877-362-8902
•

Exercise and yoga space

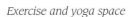

Tammy and daughter Brittany Koenig enjoy time together in the outdoors.

BECOMING AN OUTDOORS WOMAN

Stevens Point, Wisconsin

The workshop choices are unlike any mix that I've seen: Gut a pheasant or build a birdhouse. Shoot a rifle or design a wreath. Ice fish or dogsled. Camp or cook.

Everything in the curriculum heightens our connection to the outdoors. About 100 of us happily sleep in bunks, share bathrooms, eat cafeteria food and veer in different directions because of the 20 class options. These three days together seem far more like a campout or pajama party than a pampered escape with plush surroundings, but it works.

Teens to grandmas attend these Becoming an Outdoors Woman (BOW) workshops. They come from at least 40 states, Canada and New Zealand. BOW has chapters in other states and Canada.

At a 1991 conference, conservation and state agency leaders theorized that women didn't hunt, fish or otherwise get involved with the outdoors because they didn't know how. Would that change if they had a way to learn?

A one-day set of workshops was an experiment, arranged through the College of Natural Resources of the University of Wisconsin–Stevens Point. Classes filled quickly, and this is true for BOW events today.

"From day one, we offered a broad range of activities that would appeal to women" without intimidating them, says Christine Thomas, BOW founder and dean of the College of Natural Resources.

BOW deliberately mixes "nonharvest activities"—like building a quilt rack or learning to snowshoe—with shooting and fishing instruction. That means BOW attracts a wide mix of women: Some have long been at ease in camouflage attire; others prefer pink parkas.

"Be safe, have fun—and no politics," an instructor advises. "That's a BOW rule."

BOW programs involve all seasons and attract a wide demographic. Scholarships help low-income women participate. About 20,000 women attend at least one of 80 BOW events per year, and for some the experience is a life-changer.

For Linda Dightmon, named Conservation Educator of the Year by the Arizona Wildlife Federation, traveling to Wisconsin for a winter BOW event meant learning something new. An avid hunter, she borrowed winter clothing, ice fished for the first time and was thrilled to catch bluegill.

BOW teachers encourage students to explore at their own pace. The format is relaxed, conversational and goes beyond "how to" advice.

At a dog sledding session, for example, students spend 90 minutes of classroom time learning about equipment, animals and philosophy. Then they each mush solo, several times, with a team of dogs.

Teachers are a targeted BOW audience and the program tries to "help teachers better infuse environmental education into the classroom." With that come more intangible benefits, for student and teacher alike.

"We've seen women grow in self-esteem and confidence, discover new things about themselves. Instructors could see that

Take a class and learn to mush your own dog team.

WISCONSIN

Learn to survive—and enjoy!—winter camping.

WISCONSIN

they were changing lives, so it's been a fun and positive influence all around," says Christine.

Program cost depends upon the type of activities pursued. The base cost, including lodging and meals, tends to be about $250.

Becoming an Outdoors Woman
University of Wisconsin–Stevens Point
College of Natural Resources
Stevens Point, Wisconsin
www.uwsp.edu/cnr/bow 877-BOWOMAN

•

A couple of male greater prairie chickens strut their stuff.

PRAIRIE CHICKEN FESTIVAL

Stevens Point, Wisconsin

The funky dancing begins at the onset of dawn, and it is a private affair—a ritual that starts with cooing. The low hum of interplay seems almost meditative.

The guys strut like flamboyant show-offs, and the gals act like they'd rather not be bothered, yet they linger. A neck patch of brilliant orange balloons when the male mating call grows more persistent; the females remain indifferent, uncooperative.

We sit in a wooden blind that accommodates four people, and watch the courtship dance of 15 males to 2 females.

For almost three hours, we sit relatively wordless on little benches and peek out of unobtrusive holes, making sure to not reveal our silhouettes. One glimpse of an interloper, and this odd mating dance would end abruptly.

In the background are the honks, chirps and twitters of geese, meadowlarks, woodcocks, bobolinks and other feathered creatures.

Dozens of people rise in chilly darkness to watch prairie chickens prance, hop with wings aflutter, stake out and protect territory within their booming (mating) ground. The males do all the talking—called booming—about 50 feet in front of us, appearing shortly after we settle inside of our wooden nest.

Prairie chicken blind

What began as a word-of-mouth opportunity for serious birders has turned into a way to draw casual tourists into central Wisconsin for an unusual, close-to-nature experience that can't be duplicated elsewhere in the state.

For one weekend in April each year, conservationists lead nature lovers to remote wildlife management areas that contain greater prairie chickens (one of three kinds of prairie chickens in the U.S.).

Until 1955, prairie chickens could be hunted in Wisconsin. They have since been designated a protected species. The flock, which could be found in every county at the beginning of that century, today totals a few thousand. Ninety percent live in the central part of the state.

"If they're doing well, then the grasslands are doing well," says educator Jodi Wieber Hermsen. She works for the Golden Sands Resource Conservation and Development Council, a nine-county environmental agency, based in Stevens Point.

The prairie chickens are skittish, maybe even a little paranoid. They require a lot of room to roam and prefer grassland habitats with no trees. They want to be able to see all around them, and seeing nothing (as in humans or other predators) is a good thing. Mating won't happen until the birds feel comfortable enough in their surroundings.

When the female birds fly away at sunrise, it's also our signal to leave the roost, and the booming ends for another day.

•

There is a 4:30 deadline to enter the blinds, so visitors are in place before any hint of daylight. Don't get fueled up on coffee before settling into the blind for three hours. There is little you can do if nature calls.

The annual Prairie Chicken Festival takes place during Earth Day weekend. Pay a nominal fee for a wristband that allows access to nature workshops, guided hikes and the annual Wisconsin Center for the Book's Literary Bash.

To reserve a predawn spot in a blind to watch the prairie chickens, pay a separate fee, which includes breakfast cooked outdoors and access to the other festival events. Daytime grassland birding tours also require reservations.

A male tries to impress the girls with his dance steps and puffing.

Activities occur in and near Wisconsin Rapids, at Rapids Mall, Necedah National Wildlife Refuge, Historic Point Basse in Nekoosa and Buena Vista, Paul J. Olson, Mead and Sandhill wildlife areas.

Central Wisconsin Prairie Chicken Festival
1462 Strongs Avenue
Stevens Point, Wisconsin
www.prairiechickenfestival.org 715-343-6215

•

Stanton W. Mead Education and Visitor Center, S2148 Highway S,
Milladore, Wisconsin, has a LEED platinum rating, the highest grade possible.
Located in the 33,000-acre Mead Wildlife Area.
www.meadwildlife.org 715-457-6771

Mary packs only the best tomatoes for Bay Produce.

BAY PRODUCE
Superior, Wisconsin

When I get to know Mary Germinaro, it is through nods and hand signals. I point to my camera, and she grins with delight. When I take an interest in her work, she reaches for an exquisitely ripened tomato. Now both of us are grinning.

We meet at Bay Produce in Superior, in the northwestern corner of Wisconsin, where Mary's job for two decades has been filling plastic four-packs with the beefsteak Superior Tomato. Bay Produce is a part of the Challenge Center, which helps developmentally disabled adults help themselves.

About two dozen workers—including Mary, who is deaf and has cerebral palsy—attentively follow these tomatoes, grown year-round in the Bay Produce greenhouses, from seedling to packaging. The unconventional fruit makes its way into high-end restaurants, average delis, grocery stores and hospital cafeterias. Up to 100 cases (each with at least 22 tomatoes) are harvested and shipped daily.

Demand tends to exceed supply. The success of the beefsteak led to the added production of grape tomatoes and sweet peppers—red, yellow and green. So what began as a one-half-acre greenhouse project in 1990 has since tripled in size.

"It's very easy to sell our tomatoes," says Debbie Gergen, work services director. "We are recognized for our quality."

The Superior Tomato is in my salad at the New Scenic Cafe, in Two Harbors, Minnesota, and in my seafood sandwich at the Angry Trout in Grand Marais, 100 miles farther north. Bay Produce customers extend into Michigan's Upper Peninsula, and as far west as Fargo, North Dakota.

"People want to know the story behind their food," Debbie observes. "We're the safe tomato—vine ripened in a monitored environment."

Anyone—college students, first graders, vacationing families—can tour the operation, by appointment. What they see is far beyond a few rows of spindly stalks weighed down by plump bounty.

The tomato plants hang thick and high in greenhouses, neatly looping around and around, some growing 30 to 35 feet in length before younger plants replace them. The roof can open to lessen humidity. Computers regulate temperature and watering. Water is recycled; nutrients are added to whatever the hydroponic plants don't absorb, then reused.

A curtain of shade eases the impact of harsh sunlight; artificial lighting may glow 16 hours daily during the dark of winter.

Employees thin out plant leaves and fruit, so the produce that remains will grow to the optimum size. They pick tomatoes ready for shipment. All tomatoes—the perfect, the oddly shaped, those with splits and those that leave the vine too green—have a market.

Others sort the harvest by size and quality, prepare boxes for packaging, add stickers to single-sale tomatoes and peppers. They weigh the finished products, whether cases or four-packs of the beefsteaks, or eight-ounce containers of grape tomatoes.

As an on-the-job treat, employees take turns eating lunch with Henk Vandenbrink, an astute tomato grower from Holland—"the hub for tomato growing in the world," says Debbie.

She refers to Henk as "the captain of our ship" because "he knows the plants. He sets the temperature, decides when the roof opens, how many leaves need to be taken off of the plants—whatever we need for excellent production."

Bay Produce
39 N. Twenty-fifth Street East
Superior, Wisconsin
www.challenge-center.org 715-394-2771
•

See the bicycles Lance Armstrong rode to victory in seven Tours de France.

TREK BICYCLE CORPORATION

Waterloo, Wisconsin

It costs nothing to tour a part of the nation's biggest bicycle manufacturing company, best known for providing the road bikes that helped make Lance Armstrong a seven-time Tour de France winner.

Trek, in Afrikaans, a South African language, means "long journey," and the company has been on an amazing path since its work began in a barn near Waterloo, Wisconsin, in 1976. Trek's first road racing model came out in 1982, and Armstrong signed on with Trek in 1997, two years before winning his first Tour de France.

Carbon technology produces ultralight but strong bike frames that exceed aerospace standards for manufacturing. The same models on the Tour de France circuit today are sold to the public. Prices range from about $300 to $10,000.

My tour group included visitors from Switzerland and a group of elementary school students, who were far from bored. They wanted to touch the bikes, see where Trek employees work, hear how the newest Trek road bike was kept a top-secret project before its official unveiling.

We learned about the rugged trails nearby that are used for bike testing. They are too dangerous to be open to the public. Also off-limits are the test labs.

The Waterloo headquarters has an atrium whose walls are filled with yellow jerseys and bikes that Lance Armstrong used in his seven Tour de France wins. The assortment includes the bike that he crashed during the 2003 race.

In the lobby is a summary of Trek company history, which includes key bike equipment.

Trek employees dress casually, are rewarded for bicycling to work and have their own exercise room with easily more than a dozen choices of equipment.

Future contenders for the Tour de France?

Visitors must wear closed-toe shoes during one-hour Trek tours at the Waterloo headquarters and Whitewater factory (30 minutes away). Call for tour times and days.

Trek Bicycle Corporation
801 W. Madison Street
Waterloo, Wisconsin
www.trekbikes.com 920-478-2191

•

WISCONSIN

WELLSPRING
West Bend, Wisconsin

When I met farm manager Jeff Schreiber, he was taking a break from the vegetable harvest to prepare lunch for his work crew. That meant roasting brussels sprouts and simmering a pot of carrot-ginger soup. For dessert: sweet potato pie. To drink: tap water.

Simple, nourishing and down-home. This is the vibe that permeates Wellspring, an organic farm, retreat center and Hostelling International location.

As Jeff chopped and stirred, a sleek cat bounced onto my lap and licked my chin. Later, a rooster and his harem followed me on these 35 acres, 5 of which are certified organic.

Would-be yoga teachers gather here for training. Their sleeping quarters in the upper level of the retreat center (a former barn) contain a dozen twin beds and little else. At ground level are living quarters for Wellspring staff, plus up to three interns whose seven-month visits emphasize hands-on agricultural education.

Guest accommodations inside the hostel consist of one room with seven twin beds, plus a bathroom, and two pleasant bedrooms in the farmhouse.

Simple and clean accommodations are ready for yoga instructors-in-training.

Nature lovers gravitate to Wellspring to learn and work. Visitors are welcome, but only by appointment. Founder Mary Ann Ihm says the organic farm attracts many visitors, some from as far away as Pakistan, Korea and Slovakia.

Wellspring is part of the international World Wide Opportunities on Organic Farms network, whose hosts provide meals, lodging and education about sustainable agriculture in exchange for daily help with farm chores and projects.

Besides internships, Wellspring offers classes in small-scale gardening, food preservation and cooking. Some last part of one day; others involve the full growing season, garden planning to harvest. The staff of four act as mentors.

Wellspring grows about 50 kinds of vegetables (including 30 types of heirloom tomatoes). The harvest is sold as CSA shares and at farmers' markets. Some CSA customers pay for all or a part of their food by working on the farm up to four hours per week, so organic food has been accessible to all income levels—at least through the typical outdoor growing season.

Wellspring is adjacent to Riveredge Nature Center, a 370-acre refuge that skirts the Milwaukee River. The center's 10 miles of hiking trails are used for cross-country skiing in winter. The closest town, Newburg, is about a mile away.

Wellspring
4382 Hickory Road
West Bend, Wisconsin
www.wellspringinc.org 262-675-6755
•

WISCONSIN

More Green Places to Visit

The Travel Green Wisconsin (www.travelgreenwisconsin.com) voluntary business certification program began in 2007 and is considered a national leader in comprehensive ecotourism initiatives. Roughly 500 restaurants, attractions, entertainment venues and other businesses meet minimum preset standards. Lodging properties that rise to the top of this ratings system include:

Artha Sustainability Center, 9784 Highway K, Amherst. A solar-powered bed-and-breakfast on 90 acres with organic gardens, year-round renewable energy workshops and retreats.

www.arthaonline.com 715-824-3463

•

Inn Serendipity, 7843 Highway P, Browntown. A rural and laid-back escape completely powered by renewable energy. Vegetarian cuisine. Guests share the owners' farmhouse; a more rustic choice is Inn Serendipity Woods, a 30-acre wildlife sanctuary with cabin.

www.innserendipity.com 608-329-7058

•

Arbor House, 3402 Monroe Street, Madison. This model for urban ecology adds earth-friendly design to two historic structures (including one of the city's oldest homes). Room rates include use of bikes and a canoe, for exploring the adjacent University of Wisconsin Arboretum and lake.

www.arbor-house.com 608-238-2981

•

Jacks Lake B&B, New Auburn. An off-the-grid getaway, with garden or lake views for the three guest rooms. Forward-thinking radiant heating, solar power and a solar greenhouse.

www.jackslakebandb.com 715-967-2593

•

Shrooms Kitchen at River Valley Ranch, 39900 W. Sixtieth Street, Burlington, (the business actually is in unincorporated Slades Corners), works delightful miracles with mushrooms grown on the Bill and Eric Rose farm since 1976. Five types of fungi—button, shiitake, oyster, portabella, crimini—grow year-round, without chemical intervention or growth enhancers. Buy the raw ingredient or a mushroom-growing kit, or select from a wide assortment of pickled vegetables, artisan salsas and pasta sauces at the farm store. Online orders also taken.

Wild morels and oyster mushrooms

Each jar is packed by hand, and choices aren't limited to mushrooms. How about Sweet Peach Salsa or Spicy Olive Bruschetta?

www.rivervalleykitchens.com 888-711-7476

•

Sassy Cow Creamery, W4192 Bristol Road, Columbus, opened as a milk bottling operation in 2008 on the James and Robert Baerwolf farm. Now other dairy products, including ice cream, are made and sold here. "Many consumers don't know or recognize the ingredients in the food they purchase and consume," the Baerwolfs observe. "We offer an alternative to that."

The brothers farm their grandfather's land in traditional and organic ways. About 20 percent of their 500-cow herd is kept separate and pastured in organic fields, so the creamery sells both organic and conventional (but hormone-free) milk. More than a dozen ice cream flavors—from Orange Chocolate Bliss to Purple Cow (black raspberry, with chocolate chips)—are sold in varying amounts, from single scoops to three-gallon buckets.

www.sassycowcreamery.com 608-445-2010

•

Kelley Country Creamery has some surprising ice cream flavors.

Tim and Karen Kelley's 200-acre dairy farm has an extraordinary history. The family business began in 1861 on a road once home to 39 Kelley families. Today **Kelley Country Creamery**, W5215 Highway B, Fond du Lac, sells up to 20 ice cream flavors from a neat red building with a sun porch that overlooks a working farm. Expect traditional ice cream choices, along with an occasional surprise, like maple bacon, or the sharp-sweet taste of bleu cheese and pear.

www.kelleycountrycreamery.com
920-923-1715

•

Aztalan State Park is an archaeological site and National Historic Landmark east of Lake Mills, at Highways Q and B. The area was home to an ancient Middle-Mississippian village that thrived, then vanished.

www.dnr.wi.gov 920-648-8774

•

Journey Inn, W3671 200th Avenue, Maiden Rock, provides life coaching and energy therapy in addition to an environmentally friendly place to stay on 66 rural acres in a valley with a spring-fed creek. For rent are a cottage that sleeps up to six and four guest rooms in the inn.

www.journeyinn.net 715-448-2424

•

About 125 adults with disabilities have jobs because of Papa Pat's Farmhouse Recipes. About three dozen products—cookies, jams, soups, relishes, pancake mixes—are processed through the Hoden Center rehab program in Wisconsin; some of the recipes are a century old.

In 2010 the Hoden Center opened the **Wisconsin Innovation Kitchen**, 851 Dodge Street, Mineral Point, a 10,000-square-foot food-processing facility—big enough to pursue Papa Pat's work, as well as help farms and cooks develop their own food products. A retail shop, featuring products made here, is open on weekdays. Occasionally cooking classes are offered.

www.wi.innovationkitchen.org 608-987-3558
www.papapats.com 866-987-3336

•

WISCONSIN

Fortaleza Hall joins Frank Lloyd Wright's buildings at S.C. Johnson in Racine (page 196).

Participants at the annual **Woodlanders' Gathering at Shake Rag Alley Center for Arts and Crafts**, 18 Shake Rag Street, Mineral Point, gather nature-based materials to use in artwork. Shake Rag also teaches rustic arts, black-smithing, stage crafts and a host of other topics that spur creativity.

www.shakeragalley.com 608-987-3292

•

Horse lovers can bring their animal to **Spur of the Moment Ranch**, 14221 Helen Lane, Mountain. Its cabins with modern amenities and corrals are next to riding trails in Nicolet National Forest. The owners' vermiculture operation produces nutrient-rich compost from all the horse manure—enough to sell by the bag.

www.spurofthemomentranch.org 800-644-8783

•

Sunseed Eco-Education Center, 110 Notre Dame Street, Mount Calvary, hosts an annual **Dandelion Festival** in spring, to celebrate the dandelion's value as an edible plant that is nutritious to eat (and drink).

www.ssnd-milw.org 920-753-2131

•

Fortaleza Hall, Racine, isn't a Frank Lloyd Wright design but inspired by the architect's adjacent Administration Building and Research Tower for S.C. Johnson. LEED-certified, glass-paneled Fortaleza Hall is one part employee amenities (dining room, bank, fitness center, company store) and one part gallery of company history and library of Wright artifacts and literature. Full of earth-friendly features, including a vertical garden, rainwater collection, extensive use of natural lighting, sustainably harvested woods and local building materials. Open for free tours; reservations required.

www.scjohnson.com 262-260-2154

•

At **Namekagon Waters Retreat**, N8760 River Road, Trego, a roomy yurt on 37 acres easily accommodates four adults overnight in a nature-rich setting. Consider this a luxury camping experience. The yurt, a dome of canvas with a wood floor, contains homey furnishings and a wood-burning stove. Containers of water are brought in for cooking, drinking and washing. A cute, tidy outhouse is just steps away.

On the premises is a licensed masseuse whose work takes place next to a traditional Finnish sauna. You might see bald eagles nesting while your muscles are kneaded. Other diversions include a disc golf course, labyrinth, hiking trails and nearby canoeing. In winter, bring cross-country skis.

715-635-2027

•

Tetzner Dairy Products, 30455 Nevers Road, Washburn, sells vanilla, chocolate, chocolate mint and cherry ice cream sandwiches. Serve yourself and put what you owe into a payment box. Hours are roughly 7 a.m. to 9 p.m. The shed-like store is straightforward, and transactions typically are on the honor system because owner Phillip Tetzner's family is busy farming.

www.tetznerdairy.com 715-373-2330

•

Cheesemaker Brenda Jensen, who has won international awards for her soft sheep's milk cheeses, welcomes overnight guests at her 76-acre farm, **Hidden Springs Creamery**, S1597 Hanson Rd., Westby. She and her husband, Dean, plow with a team of Percheron draft horses. Donkeys protect the pastured sheep from predators.

www.hiddenspringscreamery.com 608-634-2521

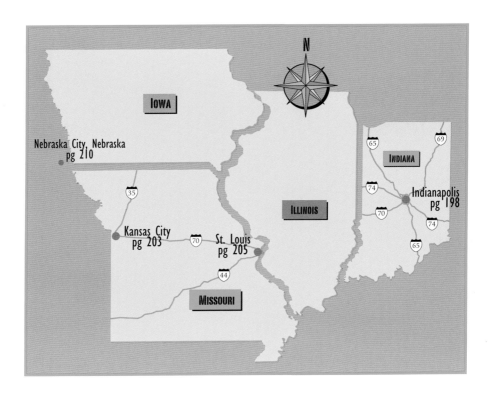

Here are four more "don't miss" cities that are notable eco-tourist destinations in the Midwest:

Indianapolis, Indiana
Kansas City, Missouri
St. Louis, Missouri
Nebraska City, Nebraska

4 MORE CITIES

You can travel by gondola or Segway to White River State Park.

WHITE RIVER STATE PARK

Indianapolis, Indiana

For years I've been a master at avoiding the Segway. Those helmet-headed drivers would look pretty dorky, I decided, if their sets of wheels went AWOL, leaving behind bruised bodies and egos. Mind you, it's not as if I ever witnessed somebody getting flipped off the machine, unless you count footage of President Bush in 2003, when he fell off a Segway because he reportedly forgot to turn it on.

Har-har, the world responded. Lord, that'll never be me, I resolved. So I long demurred whenever invited to take a Segway for a spin.

But the two-wheeled device turned out to be an ideal way to easily, efficiently and (relatively) effortlessly tour White River State Park, 250 acres of green space, canals, art and other attractions in downtown Indianapolis.

Our tour guide, Bob Whitt, the park's executive director, deadpans that Segways seldom end up sunk along the sometimes-narrow, three-mile Canal Walk

Loop. The path extends north of the park to Buggs Temple, a former gospel concert venue that today draws cocktail crowds and diners at the two restaurants (Euphoria and Creation Cafe) of the long-ago church. Along the way, we see people in rented pedal boats and surrey tandem bicycles. Others take gondola rides, jog or walk.

Indiana's only urban state park also is home to museums, a zoo and a minor league ballpark. Dozens of outdoor sculptures dot the acreage, whose sidewalks follow the White River past park benches.

All are within a walk of each other, as are several hotels and shopping, dining and entertainment options linked by bicycle path expansions.

There's a 6,000-square-foot Slow Food vegetable patch, which replaced a flower garden. The area's caregivers include Matthew Jose, who operates Big City Farms, 1.5 acres of gardens in empty city lots that generate vegetables and fruits for local restaurants and CSA shares.

"A lot of customers see what the range of produce can be in a small space, and that gets them excited about trying to grow food on their own," he says. It is the same with the White River park setting, which exists as a teaching tool and inspiration to others. Second Helpings, a community kitchen and food pantry, gets the garden harvest.

White River State Park
801 W. Washington Street
Indianapolis, Indiana
www.in.gov/whiteriver 800-665-9056
•

Also inside the park are these attractions:

Congressional Medal of Honor Memorial individually recognizes 3,449 (and counting) Americans who have received the nation's highest award for military valor.

www.medalofhonormemorial.com
•

Eiteljorg Museum of American Indians and Western Art is the only Midwest museum devoted to its subject's traditional and contemporary art, culture, history.

www.eiteljorg.org 317-636-9378
•

IMAX Theater shows larger-than-life 3D films of life, history and world exploration.

www.imaxindy.com 317-233-4629
•

Indiana State Museum has interactive exhibits that explain state history and project into the future, in a building made with indigenous materials (limestone, sandstone).

www.indianamuseum.org 317-232-1637

•

Indianapolis Zoo is known for its African elephant research and breeding and its racing cheetahs. Accredited as a zoological park, botanical garden and aquarium.

www.indianapoliszoo.com 317-630-2001

•

NCAA Hall of Champions has test-your-skill exercise areas and exhibits that showcase and archive all the sports championships that the NCAA administers.

www.ncaa.org/hall_of_champions 317-916-4255

•

Victory Field is home of the Indianapolis Indians minor league baseball team. *Sports Illustrated* called it "the best minor league ballpark in America" in 2001.

www.indyindians.com 317-269-3545

•

White River Gardens, within the zoo, is a botanical attraction with water garden, glass conservatory and walkways on 3.3 acres.

www.indianapoliszoo.com

•

Segue to Segway:

Excursions on Segways, which operate on a rechargeable electric battery, are becoming more common in urban areas. The "world's first self-balancing human transporter"—in the words of Segway founder Dean Kamen—went on sale in 2002, and now at least 200 locations globally offer city tours on them. (Even skittish folks like me can learn the basics of maneuvering a Segway within 15 minutes. Truly.)

The Segway averages 14 times less in greenhouse gas emissions than a car. Although Americans get into cars 900 million times a day, the Environmental Protection Agency says solo drivers embark on one-half of these trips, driving no more than five miles.

For more about manufacturer-authorized tours: www.segway.com

•

Floating and stationary art color 100 Acres.

More green places to visit in Indianapolis:

Eight pieces of art, whimsical to utilitarian, are on display at **100 Acres**, a parklike setting with a 35-acre lake and walking trails next to the **Indianapolis Museum of Art**, 4000 Michigan Road. Admission is free.
www.imamuseum.org 317-923-1331

•

Chef Regina Mehallick, owner of **R Bistro**, 888 Massachusetts Avenue, was among the first to invest in the city's rundown Mass Ave area, which is now a showplace for dining diversity and culture. No one produces more duck in the U.S. than Indiana, so don't be surprised to see it on her menu. The chef favors local ingredients, adding European flair in her intimate, 56-seat restaurant. Another nice touch: her little vegetable garden, in the lot next to the restaurant.
www.rbistro.com 317-423-0312

•

4 MORE CITIES

Colorful University Place follows many eco-friendly practices.

At one end of **University Place Conference Center and Hotel**, 850 W. Michigan Street, is a skywalk to Indiana University Hospital. At another end is the National Art Museum of Sport, devoted to art of and by dozens of athletes who represent at least 40 sports. This free attraction in the hotel's conference center is open on weekdays.

The AAA four-diamond hotel, on a college campus, lists dozens of green business practices and in 2010 won the Green Venue of the Year award of the Indiana chapter of Meeting Professionals International. Check out the hotel gift shop, which makes fair trade items and local products a priority.

www.universityplace.iupui.edu 317-269-9000

A working paddle wheel evokes the steamboat.

ARABIA STEAMBOAT MUSEUM

Kansas City, Missouri

When the steamboat *Arabia* hit a submerged tree in 1856 and sank in the Missouri River, about 10 miles north of Kansas City, all people on board survived. That was a relief, and little was done to retrieve the vessel's cargo of ordinary merchandise used in frontier life.

"We think of it here as a floating Walmart," explains Tyler Banks. Nothing of such great value would make it worth risking life against the muddy river's nasty currents. "At the time, there were boats like this leaving Kansas City almost every hour."

Too thick to drink and too thin to plow: This was the Missouri River's reputation. Its rhythms and route veered with the passage of time.

So the *Arabia*'s whereabouts were forgotten, the steamboat nothing more than folklore—until David Hawley decided to scour a cornfield with a strong metal detector. He had a hunch he'd find where the *Arabia* sank, based on old river maps and fleeting historical accounts. The adventure began as a treasure hunt.

"They weren't thinking about a museum but had a change of heart," says Tyler, a tour guide at the Arabia Steamboat Museum. "I think their definition of 'treasure' changed once they got onto the boat."

The Hawley family discovered axes and awls to wagon wheels and Yellow Bank pipe tobacco. Coffee beans from South America; 3.5 million seed buttons (made of hand-blown glass) from Italy.

About two-thirds of the 200 tons of findings are on display. The rest sits in storage, awaiting painstakingly careful cleaning and restoration.

The project earned attention from many circles, including wood and textile preservationists. Museum visitors watch and quiz working laboratory staff such as Judy Wright, a retired high school English teacher.

She pulls out a bolt of cotton fabric, produced by New York Mills, noting that tight packing and fabric density prevented disintegration. Besides fabric preservation, Judy pursues "the day-to-day discovery of the way individual garments are put together—there was no quality control like today," and she has learned to distinguish the habits of one seamstress from another.

"Beads from Italy, beaver pelt hats—it certainly changes your idea of what the frontier was like," she observes. About 80 percent of the merchandise was everyday necessities, and the rest classified as "international luxuries" of the era.

Arabia Steamboat Museum
400 Grand Boulevard
Kansas City, Missouri
www.1856.com 816-471-1856

•

Here's another green destination in Kansas City:

Watch a weekend cooking demonstration and tour the 12-acre "edible landscape" of Heartland Harvest Garden, inside **Powell Gardens**, 1609 NW Highway 50. Expect to see vineyards, orchards, greenhouse gardening and examples of food garden designs. The Garden Cafe uses the harvest in its menu. The Heartland Harvest is part of Powell's 915 acres of gardens and nature trails.
www.powellgardens.org 816-697-2600

•

City Museum has mastered the art of recycling in creative and playful ways.

CITY MUSEUM

St. Louis, Missouri

One of St. Louis's best attractions excels at finding new life for just about any old thing. The city's ultimate recycling project adds elements of entertainment, suspense, adventure and danger.

Imagine a school bus that looks as if it might tumble from the top of a ten-story building, not far from the rooftop Ferris wheel. Take a seat on either. Nearby, an abandoned jet seems suspended in midair.

The City Museum, a former shoe factory and warehouse, is full of secret passages and artwork made from castoff materials, thanks to the imagination of sculptor Bob Cassilly. Nimble visitors climb tunnels, swing on ropes,

You're encouraged to climb on the exhibits and see them from the inside out.

fumble through darkened caves, step up to a treehouse and gleefully slide down rollers that formerly transported shoes through the factory assembly line.

Some paths twist five stories high. Climbing happens in and out of the building. Although conspicuous signage alerts parents to potential hazards while at play—and the names of lawyers who have sued the museum because of injuries—the information seems to entice more than stifle business. Bloggers praise the place while boasting about bumps and bruises earned there.

Classify the City Museum as a rare attraction that simultaneously amazes visitors and satisfies the basic urges of at least two generations to explore and inspect hidden pathways. Discarded heating coils from a brewery are big enough to squirm into, then use as steps. From a distance, it's like watching people maneuver inside a giant Slinky that bends and ascends but doesn't actually move.

"There are three tunnels and over 100 feet of crawl space in the whale alone," co-owner David Jump reports. He is referring to the massive Bowhead Whale sculpture that meshes with the museum's World Aquarium, where living sea life is studied amid artsy nautical forms and elaborate excavations.

The work to create new exhibits and climbing channels is ongoing, so City Museum won't seem stale to repeat visitors. Picture giant dragonflies made out of old watchbands, a ceiling fringe made of hundreds of old neckties, mosaics of junkyard scraps (which my guide refers to as "foreign object debris").

Daredevils enroll in circus skill classes, learning trapeze or wire walking. Creative spirits emerge with unique souvenirs, made spontaneously in a glittery and cluttered Art City workshop.

The nonprofit Project for Public Spaces, based in New York, includes City Museum on its list of Great Public Spaces in the World, describing it as "an adventurous, ramshackle collection of outsized sculptures and play spaces, including famous multi-story slides."

Couples on dates, and perhaps parents who want to calm their nerves, lounge at Beatnik Bob's, whose carnival theme includes a corndogs-through-the-ages exhibit, or order a drink at the Cabin Inn, an 1804 log cabin on City Museum's ground floor.

The third floor is as somber as the museum gets. On show is an unusual assortment of architectural artifacts, accompanied by the often-sad tales of demolition undertaken in the name of progress. Notice the remnants from architect Louis Sullivan buildings.

Bargain hunters find their way to the Baleout, a fourth-floor clothing resale shop touted as among the biggest in the Midwest. Inventory arrives in one-ton bales and prices are paltry: from $1 for a coat, $2 for a tuxedo bow tie.

One can only imagine what sits in museum archives and storage. Next up for the museum founder is transformation of an old cement factory, a work-in-progress since the 1990s.

City Museum
701 N. Fifteenth Street
St. Louis, Missouri
www.citymuseum.org
314-231-2489
•

A frilled lizard made of junk pieces adorns a column.

More green places to visit in St. Louis:

A LEED-level upgrade at the herbarium inside **Missouri Botanical Garden**, 4344 Shaw Boulevard, resulted in about $100,000 in annual savings, with energy use nearly cut in half. The building's millions of plants include some collected by Charles Darwin. The garden's restaurant, Sassafras, was the first in Missouri to gain Green Restaurant Association certification.

www.mobot.org 314-577-5100

•

A Farmers Platter and a flight of beers make a delicious meal at Schlafly Bottleworks.

Tour **Schlafly Bottleworks**, 7260 Southwest Avenue, and sample the handcrafted beer that competes well with the city's big dog, Anheuser-Busch. Also on the Schlafly premises is a well-tended garden, whose bounty (about 3,600 pounds of veggies per season) goes into the brewpub's daily specials. Add an order of warm pretzel bread from Companion Bakery, with a beer-cheese sauce for dipping, or make a meal out of the Farmers Platter, a mix of local sausages and spent grain beer bread.

On Wednesday afternoons during the growing season, a farmers' market with about three dozen vendors moves onto the premises. Local, family-owned purveyors get star treatment on the brewpub menu. Special dinners seat up to 80 and put the spotlight on local ingredients, one farm at a time.

www.schlafly.com 314-241-BEER

•

Order a BLT salad, meat loaf platter or slow-cooked corned beef at **McMurphy's Grill**, 614 N. Eleventh Street, and contribute to a worthy cause. Since 1990, the restaurant has provided job training to homeless and mentally ill adults—the first such program in the U.S.

St. Patrick Center oversees this endeavor and supports clientele work in other ways, including the **City Seeds Urban Farm**, mentored by the nonprofit **Gateway Greening**. Look for the bounty—which includes a dwarf fruit tree orchard—growing near Union Station.

www.stpatrickcenter.org 314-231-3006
www.gatewaygreening.org 314-588-9600

Environmental awareness is a decades-old priority at Lied Lodge.

LIED LODGE AND CONFERENCE CENTER

Nebraska City, Nebraska

Douglas fir timbers stretch upward for three stories in the spacious and warmly lit lobby of Lied Lodge. Proverbs and inspirational messages are chiseled or stenciled on walls; the effect is dramatic and welcoming.

A two-sided stone fireplace reaches the rafters, too, making this a perfect place to lounge with a spouse or a book as soft jazz drifts from a nearby piano. Regional artists perform throughout the year.

Beyond the patio doors of some guest rooms, and the lobby's generous windows, is a sweeping view of Arbor Day Farm and Arbor Lodge State Historical Park.

Lied Lodge offers prime seating for lovers of wildlife, who may spot red fox, white-tailed deer or wild turkey from their indoor or veranda perch. The more energetic can follow the walking trails. Horse-drawn carriage rides cut through the lodge arboretum, whose 50-plus species of trees include apple and hazelnut orchards.

Lied Lodge Greenhouse has led the world in the production of hazelnut seedlings. On the adjacent **Arbor Day Farm** are trees that produce 165 kinds of apples, many of them heirloom varieties.

The harvest from these trees is woven into the lodge's restaurant menu. Apple chips subtly flavor meats in the on-premises smokehouse. One Wolf River apple, the size of a small pumpkin, is enough to fill a pie.

The 144-room Lied Lodge, which began as a resource for the National Arbor Day Foundation, makes environmental awareness and practices a priority. Wood chips from quick-growing poplar trees heat the building and the swimming pool. The fuelwood plant also powers the central air system and laundry equipment. The Visitors Gallery explains how this happens. Carpeting is made of recycled plastic bottles, carpet padding from recycled tires, and light shades and sconces from recycled paper.

The lodge and adjacent farm share a mission: "inspiring people to plant, nurture and celebrate trees."

Lied Lodge and Conference Center
2700 Sylvan Road
Nebraska City, Nebraska
www.liedlodge.org 800-546-5433

•

4 MORE CITIES

Trade goods recovered and restored from the steamboat Arabia *(page 203).*

INDEX

N

PHOTO AND TEXT CREDITS

Photographs and text by Mary Bergin, except as noted:

Page viii	Amy Lynn Schereck photo
Page 6, 10, back cover	John Mather photos
Page 8	EyeWire photo
Page 22	Text originally written for *Madison Magazine*
Page 48	Jack Bartholmai photo
Page 95	EyeWire photo
Page 112	Troy Melhus photo, Minnesota Twins Baseball
Page 113	Wayne Kryduba photo, Minnesota Twins Baseball, and Meet Minneapolis
Page 146	Text originally written for *AAA Living* magazine
Page 166	Brent Nicastro photo
Page 180	Text originally written for *Wisconsin Trails* magazine
Pages 64, 67,183,185	Flying Fish Graphics photos
Page 186	Text originally written for *Edible Madison* magazine

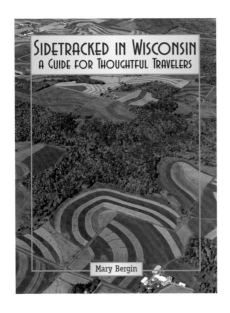

Other Books by Mary Bergin

SIDETRACKED IN WISCONSIN
A Guide for Thoughtful Travelers

A guide for the curious traveler, willing to be sidetracked and experience something quirky, interesting, and unusual. Maps, road trips, lodging, restaurants, hikes, museums, taverns, tours, theaters, and index.

ISBN 978-0-9761450-4-2 $23.00

•

HUNGRY FOR WISCONSIN
A Tasty Guide for Travelers

Here's a guide for the hungry traveler, looking for wonderful culinary experiences or familiar and favorite comfort foods. Restaurants, festivals, tours, taverns, recipes, road trips, and index.

ISBN 978-0-9815161-0-3 $25.00

•

www.itchycatpress.com
Read about Mary Bergin's travels at **www.roadstraveled.com**.